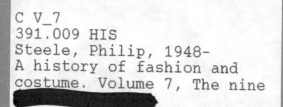

A History of Fashion and Costume

Volume 7
The Nineteenth Century

Philip Steele

☑® Facts On File, Inc.

The Nineteenth Century

Copyright © 2005 Bailey Publishing Associates Ltd

Produced for Facts On File by
Bailey Publishing Associates Ltd
11a Woodlands
Hove BN3 6TJ

Project Manager: Roberta Bailey
Editor: Alex Woolf
Text Designer: Simon Borrough
Artwork: Dave Burroughs, Peter Dennis,
Tony Morris
Picture Research: Glass Onion Pictures
Consultant: Tara Maginnis, Ph.D.
Associate Professor of the University of Alaska,
Fairbanks, and creator of the website, The
Costumer's Manifesto (http://costumes.org/).

Printed and bound in Hong Kong.

Facts On File, Inc.
132 West 31st Street
New York NY 10001

Facts On File books are available at special
discounts when purchased in bulk quantities for
businesses, associations, institutions, or sales
promotions. Please call our Special Sales
Department in New York at 212/967-8800 or
800/322-8755.
You can find Facts On File on the World Wide
Web at: http://www.factsonfile.com

**Library of Congress
Cataloging-in-Publication Data**

Steele, Philip, 1948–
A history of fashion and costume.
Volume 7, The Nineteenth
Century/Philip Steele
    p. cm.
Includes bibliographical references and
    index.
    ISBN 0-8160-5950-0
    1. Clothing and dress—History—
19th century. 2. Fashion—History—
19th century.
    GT595.S74 2005
    391/.009/034—dc 22
2005049453

The publishers would like to thank
the following for permission to use
their pictures:

Art Archive: 17 (bottom), 19, 21 (top),
22, 23 (left), 24 (both), 27 (top), 28
(top), 35, 38, 39 (both), 40, 41 (both),
43, 44, 47, 56 (bottom), 57.
Bridgeman Art Library: 6 (left), 7, 9,
12, 13, 16, 21 (bottom), 26 (top), 29,
30, 36, 37, 42, 50, 52, 53, 55, 56 (top),
58.
Mary Evans Picture Library: 10, 32,
45.
Peter Newark: 6 (right), 15, 17 (top).
Topham: 54 (left).
Werner Forman Archive: 14.
Victoria & Albert Museum: 25, 31
(top), 34, 48, 49 (top), 51, 54 (right).

Contents

Introduction   5

Chapter 1: In the New World   6

Chapter 2: Europe: Nations and Costumes   22

Chapter 3: Western Dress: at Work and Play   32

Chapter 4: Empires and Colonies   44

Timeline   60

Glossary   61

Further Information   63

Index   64

Introduction

The nineteenth century was a time of great social change. The world was opening up, thanks to railroads, steamships, and new roads. Trade became global. New technology allowed huge, noisy cotton mills in cities such as Manchester, England, to turn out vast quantities of cloth, which could then be sold around the world. Factories and mills replaced cottages and small workshops.

In America, bustling new cities were swollen by an incoming tide of immigrants from Europe. Back in the Old World, the most powerful European nations built up overseas empires in Africa, Asia, Australia, and the Pacific islands. As a result, European dress, often most unsuitable for the local climate, could now be seen from Cape Town to Shanghai.

This book looks at developments in fashion and costume during the century, and how they were influenced by changes in people's lives, both at work and play.

In many places, costume did not change very much, and the local peoples still made and wore splendid regional costumes—furs, feathers, silks, or embroidered cottons—as their everyday clothing. This great diversity would soon change, however, as a result of mass-produced, machine-woven cloths and chemical dyes.

The nineteenth century is a comparatively recent period in history. In museums and exhibitions, the actual costumes people wore at that time can still be seen. Pictures of these costumes can be viewed in fashion plates from old magazines, and engravings or early photographs from every corner of the world.

Chapter 1: In the New World

The population of the Americas in the nineteenth century was made up of very many ethnic and cultural groups. Each had its own traditions of clothing, and within these there were many variants defined by region, class, age, wealth, or profession.

This was a society on the move. Existing groups were constantly added to and enriched by immigration into the New World, mostly from Europe, including Italians, Germans, Poles, Swedes, Russians, Jews, and Irish people. In the course of the century, one could also find Chinese immigrants in California, Southeast Asians in Guyana (then British Guiana), and Asian Indians on Caribbean islands such as Trinidad.

Native Americans

Indigenous peoples of the Americas, then referred to fairly universally as "Indians," still inhabited the continent from the Arctic Ocean to the southern tip of South America, although few remained in those areas which had already been heavily settled by Europeans. In many areas, native peoples still wore magnificent traditional dress, made from skins, furs, feathers, and textiles of natural fibers.

European contact with Native Americans was characterized by violence and warfare, but also by trade. Western items of dress or decoration were often adopted, such as beads, coins, blankets, jackets, coats, or hats. Often native peoples were forced to wear European dress.

European Americans

Some European immigrants to American cities wore clothes or fashions unique to their nationality or religion. However, most new city dwellers wore the standard European fashions or working costumes of their day.

Throughout the century, the United States grew as an independent nation, acquiring vast new tracts of land by purchase, treaty, or invasion. Settlers moved west. In Canada, too, European farmers moved onto the prairies. In South America, new

The Sioux chief Black Rock painted by George Catlin (1796–1872). Between 1832 and 1840 this Pennsylvania-born artist made 470 paintings recording the dress and customs of Native Americans.

"Uncle Sam," personifying the United States, welcomes immigrants with open arms. This cartoon dating from 1880 shows Irish, Russians, and Italians in supposed national costume.

waves of migrants colonized remote regions such as Patagonia. Across the Americas, pioneers of European or mixed descent were building settlements and farms, mining, logging, and building railroads.

City clothing was rarely appropriate in these wide open spaces, where the only means of transport was horseback. Fur trappers, lumberjacks, cowboys, miners, and engineers all had to wear appropriate dress for a tough, active life. So, too, did sailors, who packed their few clothes and possessions into small sea chests. Tall-masted sailing ships rounded Cape Horn, bound for San Francisco, or sailed out of New England to hunt whales.

African-Americans

The first African-Americans were slaves brought to South America, the Caribbean islands, and the American South in the sixteenth century. They were cruelly treated, and forced to work on sugar or cotton plantations. Their freedom was finally gained in the nineteenth century. Slavery ended in the British Caribbean in 1838, in the United States in 1865, and in

Brazil in 1888. Even then it was generally replaced by a poverty-stricken existence as sharecroppers, laborers, or fishermen. In the United States, some African-Americans made it out west and worked as cowboys. African-American dress was essentially European, but some African traditions survived.

This painting of 1847 by George Caleb Bingham shows the broad-brimmed hats, loose shirts, working trousers, and boots worn by raftsmen.

A Stitch in Time

The nineteenth century was an age of new technology. The first working sewing machine was patented in France in 1830, by Barthélemey Thimonnier, and used to make army uniforms in the 1840s. It was in the United States, however, that this invention really took off. It was developed by various inventors, including Allen B. Wilson, Walter Hunt, and Elias Howe. However, the man who came to dominate the United States and then the world market was New York-based Isaac Merritt Singer (1811–75). Singer sewing machines were soon to be found in every garment workshop and well-off home.

City Fashions in the United States

For most of the nineteenth century, the clothes to be seen on the streets of Boston, New York City, Philadelphia, or Washington did not look very different from those in London, Paris, or Berlin. A standard, international style of dress was beginning to appear.

In the 1800s

Women's fashions of the 1800s were some of the most elegant – yet comfortable and natural looking – that the century would see. Straight-cut ankle-length dresses were made of fine embroidered muslin or of sturdier printed cottons. They were high waisted, with a ribbon below the bosom and short, puffed sleeves. Arm-length gloves might be worn for an elegant ball, and hands could be kept warm inside a fur muff on cold winter afternoons. Shoes were flat, dainty leather slippers.

In this period, men stopped wearing knee-length breeches and stockings and began to wear long trousers. A gentleman would wear a high-collared shirt with a stock wound around the neck, sometimes tied with a bow. A colorful tailcoat might be worn, reaching the backs of the knees, but cut to waist level at the front. This might be worn open to display a vest. Men might wear knee-length boots or flat slippers, sometimes with gaiters.

Mid-Century

In the 1820s and 1830s, women's skirts became increasingly full and decorated with floral trimmings and bows. By the 1850s, this style had developed into the full crinoline, whose wide, bell-like skirts were pushed out by hoops of steel and whalebone. Hair was worn pulled back from the face or curled into tight ringlets. A lady might carry a parasol.

Men's dress became more sober, favoring black jackets, although checkered or striped trousers were still quite common. Cravats and neckties worn in a loose bow were worn over white shirts with high collars. Hair was worn with sideburns, extensive whiskers, or full beards.

From the 1870s

In the 1870s and 1880s, the skirts of women's dresses became narrower again. A "fishtail," or short train, was worn for a while and a pad or frame called a bustle was worn at the rear of a tight skirt to exaggerate the backside. The

American men's day wear of the 1850s is shown on the left, and formal evening wear on the right.

Bonnets and Top Hats

Young ladies of the early 1800s wore straw hats or bonnets, often decorated with flowers and tied with a ribbon under the chin. Larger round bonnets, trimmed with lace and ribbons, were worn in mid-century. By the 1870s, hats were replacing bonnets for the most fashionable ladies—perhaps a pillbox tipped forward at a jaunty angle and topped with feathers or artificial cherries.

Out west, broad-brimmed hats provided shelter from the sun and wind, but in the cities, men wore hats with narrower brims and higher crowns. In the mid-century, the top hat, a tall black cylinder with a narrow brim was standard city wear. Rounded felt hats with a low crown were often worn by men from the 1860s onward. By the late 1880s, smart round hats with a narrow upturned brim, known as derbies, were popular with all classes.

narrow-waisted look was created with the help of laced whalebone corsets, often worn so tight that they gave the wearer medical problems. At the same time, short jackets and blouses began to be worn with long skirts. Buttoned boots became popular.

By the end of the century, men's everyday suits were beginning to resemble their modern form, with a jacket reaching below the waist, and trousers. Fancy gold or silver chains, often decorated with dangling coins and draped across the chest, were attached to a watch kept in the vest pocket.

Back East

The northeast was the most urbanized part of the United States in the nineteenth century. It was a center of industry, business—and of fashion. The women of New York City wore the most elaborate finery, admiring illustrations of bonnets, bows, and the latest Paris fashions in magazines such as *Godey's Lady's Book* (founded in 1830).

All classes aspired to be smart, and the less wealthy repaired and altered secondhand clothes to keep up with fashion. It was increasingly difficult to tell people's class or trade from their style of dress alone, although the quality of the clothing generally revealed the truth.

The Garment Industry

The northeast was a center of the textile trade. Ready-made clothing became an important industry from the 1830s onward, starting with the production of men's trousers and jackets and women's cloaks.

Standardized sizes appeared in the 1860s.

The manufacture of textiles and garments provided jobs for women and provided a major source of employment for immigrant labor. However, the fashions that clothed nineteenth-century America were produced at great social cost. In the 1830s, women at the Lowell cotton mills in Massachusetts worked an eighty-one-hour week for three dollars, out of which they had to pay the company for their board and lodging.

In the New York City garment trade, sweatshops, child labor, and unequal pay for women were common practice. As a result, women tailors, shoemakers, laundry workers, and umbrella-makers formed some of the first labor unions in the United States. A major protest by New York City garment workers on March 8th, 1857 was broken up by police. Since

The original bloomers represented the first attempt by American feminists to introduce practical clothing. Even this modest reform caused outrage.

Bloomers

Amelia Jenks was born at Harper, New York, in 1818. In 1849, at Seneca Falls, she founded a feminist magazine called *The Lily*. One of her collaborators was Elizabeth Cady Stanton, who was irritated by the impractical nature of women's fashion. Stanton, the actress Fanny Kemble, and others began to wear a shorter bell-shaped dress over baggy "pantalettes" gathered at the ankle. This outraged conservative opinion. Amelia rushed to defend clothing reform in her magazine. Soon her articles became notorious and the pantalettes were nicknamed "bloomers," Bloomer being Amelia's married name. Irritated by the controversy, the women gave up wearing bloomers. However, dress reform for women was now on the agenda, and became an increasingly important issue after Amelia's death in 1894.

An east coast beauty promenades at the seaside in about 1870, carrying a parasol. Her dress echoes both waves and seashells.

1910, March 8th has been commemorated around the world as International Women's Day.

Plain and Simple

The fashionable frippery of the big cities had stern critics. Many of the religious groups which had settled in regions such as Pennsylvania since the 1600s continued to dress modestly. The Quakers and the Shakers admired simplicity and plain colors in clothing, and frowned on corsetry and gaudy clothes. Another sect, the Amish, observed a strict dress code. The austere, practical costumes they wear to this day include homemade ankle-length dresses, aprons, shawls, capes, and bonnets for women and girls, and black vests and jackets over plain shirts for men and boys.

Needles and Pins

Outside the cities, most people owned few clothes beyond their practical working outfits and their Sunday best. People were thrifty, and clothes would be repeatedly repaired and mended. Young girls practiced needlework from an early age, trying out stitches and embroidery skills on samplers. Housewives made beautiful quilts, household linens, shawls, shirts, and dresses by hand.

The American South

In the early 1800s, the frontiers of the United States were expanding rapidly. Backwoodsmen, wearing buckskins and furs, were settling in the southern Appalachian mountains. With the Louisiana Purchase of 1803, France sold the vast territories of the Mississippi valley to the United States. Spain ceded Florida in 1819. Texas was annexed from the Mexicans in 1845.

While the northeastern United States was soon to undergo rapid industrial development in much the same way as northern Europe, the American South remained largely rural. Southern cotton plantations, which used slave labor, supplied the textile mills of the world. This led to economic rivalry with the north and a clash of ideals, culminating in the bloody Civil War of 1861–65, which ended slavery, but not racial discrimination.

On the Plantations

The wealthy slave owners lived in style, in splendid colonial mansions. They dressed in long tailcoats, trousers, and top hats, as seen in northern cities. The ladies wore the latest bonnets, lace, and crinolines and were famed as "southern belles." The plantation overseers might wear short jackets, vests, and low-crowned hats with broad brims.

Some slaves worked as servants indoors, while others toiled in the cotton fields. The former obtained better-quality clothing. Dress might consist of short jackets, loose shirts, and white cotton trousers for the men, with broad-brimmed straw hats. Women might wear cotton dresses or full skirts—white or brightly colored—and head scarves, often wrapped around the head as a turban. Many slaves wore cast-off clothes. In the later nineteenth century, the many poverty-stricken African-Americans who left to seek work in the northern cities wore standard city dress.

The Trail of Tears

Native Americans had managed to survive in the South, despite the loss of land and centuries of attack by settlers. Their people included the Catawba, Caddo, Choctaw, Yuchi, Seminole, Creek, and Cherokee. The Indian Removal Act of 1830 authorized the enforced removal of

The Seminole leader Osceola (Rising Sun) wears a knee-length tunic. Seminole fabrics in the nineteenth century included buckskin and cotton. Adornments included turkey and egret feathers, woolen tassels, and beadwork patterned like rattlesnake skin.

The dress of both slave-owners and slaves is shown in this painting of 1852.

Frills decorate the dress of this "southern belle." She carries the first Confederate (southern) flag, known as the "Stars and Bars."

Native Americans to regions west of the Missouri River, a tragic and brutal expulsion that became known to the Cherokee nation as the Trail of Tears.

In these troubled times, many Native Americans from the South wore European dress, but regional costume traditions also continued. For example, Seminole men might wear loose cotton shirts with appliquéd colored strips, beadwork belts, and buckskin leggings. A cloth was tied around the head, turban-style. Seminole women of the late nineteenth century wore full skirts in colored strips of cotton, and multi-stranded bead necklaces.

Masquerades and Mardi Gras

New Orleans in the nineteenth century was a lively city. French and English were spoken and it was home to riverboat men, businessmen, gamblers, drinkers, and prostitutes. Each year, the city celebrated Mardi Gras, or "Fat Tuesday," the high point of the old carnival held in Catholic Europe. At Mardi Gras, the citizens of New Orleans dressed up in spectacular costumes for parades and masked balls.

Black people were at first excluded from the festivities by white racists, but masquerades were also an old West African tradition. By the end of the nineteenth century, New Orleans was beginning to pulse with the sounds of black "jazz" musicians and the chanting and dancing of African-Americans calling themselves "Indians," dressed in elaborate feathered and beaded costumes.

Plains and Mountains

In the mid-nineteenth century, nearly a quarter of a million Native Americans lived on the Great Plains, which stretched westward to the Rocky Mountains. Some lived by farming, but most were buffalo hunters.

Feathers and Moccasins

Dress detail defined the separate identity of each plains tribe, but they had common elements. Men wore fringed shirts and buckskin leggings, while women wore long dresses. Both sexes wore slippers called moccasins. Intricate quillwork and beadwork decorated clothes and possessions, and both men and women wore their hair long, often in braids.

A short breechclout (loincloth) might be all that was worn by warriors in battle, when the face and body might be painted with clay, charcoal, dye from berries, or buffalo blood. Rank and battle honors were indicated by feathers of crow, eagle, or buzzard worn in the hair. Chiefs wore magnificent feather headdresses or war bonnets, sometimes adorned with buffalo horns or decorated with horsehair, fur, or porcupine quills. Breastplates of bone, beads, and porcupine quills were worn on the chest.

All thirty-two native peoples of the Great Plains wore leather moccasins. Many, like this pair made by the Sioux, were beautifully decorated with beadwork, dye, or tassels.

Chaps and Cowboy Boots

In the 1870s, huge herds of cattle needed to be driven out from Texas, and across the Great Plains to the new railheads, for transportation to the stockyards of Chicago. This was the age of the cowboy. It lasted for just twenty years, but became part of American legend.

Cowboy clothes were based on those of the Mexican equivalent, the *vaquero* (a word which became buckaroo in English). Tough trousers would be covered with leather "chaps" (from *chaparrerjos*) as a protection against thorny bushes. Pointed boots with a high heel were designed to stay in the stirrup. A loose shirt was worn beneath a knotted neckerchief, which could be tied over the mouth or face as protection against dust. Cowboy hats were a shorter-brimmed version of the broad Mexican sombrero. Manufacturer J. B. Stetson designed the first Western hat bearing his name in 1863. The cowboy's standard equipment included a gun belt and holster, and a rope, or "lariat," tied to the saddle.

Rolling West

Between the 1840s and 1890s, the United States relentlessly extended its territory westward, annexing Native American lands through warfare and settlement. By the 1860s, some 400,000 whites had settled on the Great Plains. Covered wagons hauled by oxen crossed the prairie grasslands and beyond, following established routes such as the trail from Independence, Missouri, to Oregon. By 1867, a railroad linked the Atlantic and Pacific Oceans.

The newcomers were farmers, prospectors, miners, hunters, trappers, railroad engineers, traders, and outlaws. They were mostly from poor backgrounds, used to lives of hardship. They owned simple clothes of wool, linen, or cotton. Women wore ankle-length dresses or full skirts, aprons, shawls, cloaks, and large cloth bonnets. Men wore shirts, jackets and coats, trousers, leather boots, and broad-brimmed felt hats.

The trappers in remote mountain regions, or professional buffalo hunters on the Plains, sometimes adopted items of Native American dress, wearing fringed buckskin jackets, furs, feathers, or beaded belts. So too did individuals within the United States Cavalry, when fighting during the Indian Wars in the 1860s and 1870s. Their regular uniform consisted of a dark blue jacket or coat, light blue trousers, gauntlets, boots and spurs, a leather sword belt, and a gun belt. Irregular outfits included straw hats, buckskin jackets, civilian shirts, and beaded knife sheaths.

A wagon train halts for the night. Desert sand, rain, mud, thorn, and saddle all took their toll on the clothing of the migrants.

West to the Pacific

Northwestern Culture

Peoples south of the Canadian border included the Southern Coast Salish and the Makah, who lived by whaling and fishing. They used cedar wood, not only for building their villages, but to make conical hats against rain and sea spray. The pliable bark of the cedar was stripped, beaten, soaked, made into yarn, and woven on upright looms into fringed skirts and blankets, worn as cloaks. Here too, white settlement saw the introduction of traded cloth, and Western dress was widespread by 1900.

California

California, originally colonized by Spanish ranchers, was ceded to the United States by Mexico in 1848. The Native Americans of California, such as the Karok, Miwok, Hupa, and Pomo, belonged to another culture. Men wore buckskin kilts and feathered headdresses. Important women of the Miwok wore cloaks of goose feathers and shell earrings. As white settlement of California increased, those peoples that survived adopted the dress of the newcomers.

The Forty-Niners

In 1845, San Francisco was a town of about four hundred people. By 1860 it was home to fifty thousand. This

The gold miners of California wore tough, working clothes to scramble through canyons and pan for gold in mountain streams.

Clothes for the Working Man

Today, jeans are worn as casual wear by men and women around the world. However, they were originally made as working clothes in California in 1850, during the Gold Rush.

Their maker was a Jewish immigrant from Bavaria called Levi Strauss. Back east in New York City, Strauss decided that he was far more likely to make his fortune by supplying the miners than by prospecting for gold himself. He therefore brought bales of heavy-duty cotton cloth to California, intending to make tents and coverings for wagons. Unable to gain a foothold in this market, he turned instead to manufacturing trousers out of the cloth. In 1874, he and Jacob Davis patented the idea of strengthening the trousers with metal rivets. These true jeans were called waist-overalls and sold at thirteen dollars and fifty cents for a dozen pairs.

Mexican, European, and Chinese dress could all be seen in a San Francisco saloon during the Gold Rush of 1849.

rapid growth was due to gold, discovered in California in 1848. Within a year, prospectors and miners, known as forty-niners for the year 1849, were pouring in from all over the world in the desperate hope of making a fortune. Most failed. They led a rough, tough life and their clothes were often worn out, tattered, and unwashed. They wore broad-brimmed felt hats, knee-length leather boots, and overcoats.

The port of San Francisco was soon home to bankers, laborers, storekeepers, sailors, sea captains, saloon bars, and showgirls. They wore all kinds of dress, depending on their trade and ethnic origin. There were European immigrants, East Coast Americans and Southerners, African-Americans, and Chinese immigrants. Many of the latter continued to wear the costumes of their homeland, such as long cotton tunics and slippers, with the men's hair bound into a long pigtail down the back. Some moved south to Los Angeles, a town which grew rapidly after the railroad arrived in the 1880s.

Southwestern Peoples

The deserts and pueblos (mud-built villages) of New Mexico and Arizona were home to Southwestern peoples, such as the Apache, Navajo, and Hopi. Typical southwestern dress included headbands and bandanas, breechclouts, woven or knitted woolen dresses, squirrel-skin shirts, and sandals or calf-length moccasins. Using an upright loom, Navajo women produced fine tapestry-woven blankets.

These armed Apache scouts, employed by the United States Cavalry in Arizona in 1880, have adopted European dress, but wear their hair long in the Native American style.

Across the North

Northern North America saw many of the same contrasts between the traditional cultures and costumes of its native peoples and those of European newcomers.

The vast lands of Canada formed a part of the British Empire until 1867, when it became self-governing. Greenland was a Danish colony. Alaska was a Russian-owned territory in the early nineteenth century, with its capital at Sitka. The Russians had come looking for furs, so beavers, seals, and sea otters were killed in huge numbers for the hat and clothing trade. Russia sold the territory to the United States in 1867.

In the 1870s, this Canadian sergeant in the Northwest Mounted Police wears a pillbox, rather than the wide-brimmed hat for which the force later became famous.

Scarlet Jackets

One of the most famous uniforms worn in North America in the late nineteenth century was that of the Northwest Mounted Police (forerunner of the Royal Canadian Mounted Police). The "Mounties" brought peace to remote, lawless regions of Canada. They wore a simple "Norfolk" (belted) jacket in scarlet, to distinguish themselves—in border regions— from the United States Cavalry. Breeches were of gray cloth, or sometimes of fawn corduroy. The hat was a blue pillbox, with a yellow or gold band and a chinstrap. In the saddle, many officers adopted a broad-brimmed felt hat, but this did not become standard issue until 1901.

Arctic Furs

Arctic peoples dressed to survive bitterly cold winter temperatures and freezing sea water. The Aleuts, natives of the Aleutian Islands, were hunters, fishers, and whalers. They wore sealskin, furs, and hooded waterproof suits made of animal intestines, with high leather boots. Peaked caps or eyeshades were made of wood.

Arctic shores from northern Alaska, across Canada to Greenland, were peopled by various groups of the Eskimo language group, including Inuit, Yupik, and Inupiaq. They made shirts of bird skins and trousers from the fur of polar bears or arctic foxes. Hooded jackets (*kooletah*) were of caribou fur. Women wore thigh-length boots (*kamiks*) of sealskin, while men's boots were often knee high. Socks were of soft hare skin or woven grass. Necklaces were of bone, and some men wore labrets (lip plugs).

Seashore, Forest, and Lake

The Northwestern culture wore similar costumes to those on the Pacific coast of Canada and southern Alaska. Cedar bark was twined or woven into blankets and skirts. Dog hair, mountain goat wool, beaver fur, caribou skin, sealskin, and traded cloth were also used. Tlingit men wore large nose rings and beautifully patterned ceremonial blankets.

Across the rest of Canada, eastward to Labrador, were the peoples of the forests and lakes, such as the Slavey, Beaver, and Cree, and northernmost

FIRST COMMUNICATION with the NATIVES of PRINCE REGENTS BAY, as Drawn by IOHN SACKHEOUSE and Presented to CAPᵀ ROSS, Augᵗ. 10.1818.

London. Published Feb.ʸ 1.1819. by John Murray, Albemarle Street.

representatives of America's Northeastern and Plains Indian cultures. Tunics and fringed trousers were made of caribou skin, moose fur, and beaver pelts. Clothes might be beaded or painted with decorative patterns. Snowshoes of interlaced rawhide were widely used in winter.

European Canada

European settlers, principally of English, Scottish, or French descent, lived in the far south of Canada, where the climate was less severe. In cities such as Montreal, Quebec, and Ontario, or in the farms of the Saint Lawrence valley, the fashions were the same as one might see in Britain, France, or the United States. The dress of the 1850s is today recreated at the oldest house in Kitchener, Ontario, which once belonged to German-born Joseph Schneider, a member of the Mennonites (a sect similar to the Amish). Here one can see the long dresses, pinafores, aprons, lace caps and bonnets of the day, alongside the domestic spinning wheel.

In more remote regions, there were fur trappers, many of them of mixed French and native descent, known as Métis. They wore fur caps, buckskins, and heavy coats. Broad-brimmed hats and boots, the standard nineteenth century dress of the pioneer, were worn by railroad workers and the prairie settlers of the 1880s, many from eastern and central Europe.

The Klondike Gold Rush of 1898 attracted a million fortune hunters to remote Yukon territory. Some of them were old-timers, but others arrived in city clothing, woefully unprepared for the snowy mountain passes.

John Ross, a British naval captain, wears full dress uniform to meet a band of Polar Eskimos in 1818. They are dressed in hooded jackets, breeches, and boots made of furs and skins.

Central and South America

In Central and South America, fashions worn by those of European and mixed descent were broadly similar to those of the United States and Europe. However, specific Spanish and Portuguese influences were still to be seen in many cities of Latin America, such as Rio de Janeiro in Brazil, or Buenos Aires in Argentina. For example, women might wear veils of black silk, or lace mantillas secured by high, ornamental tortoiseshell combs. As the nations of the region became independent, and new waves of European immigrants arrived, more workaday clothing styles became common.

Brazil's African slaves, often treated with great cruelty, wore little more than cotton shifts, trousers or skirts, and head cloths. After liberation in 1888, many left the plantations and headed for the cities.

Sombreros and Bandanas

Mexican ranch owners and vaqueros wore leather boots and often a wide-

Right:
A fashionable woman of Buenos Aires in the 1830s, wearing a Spanish-style gown and silk veil or mantilla.

brimmed felt sombrero. Peasants might dress in a shirt and loose trousers of white cotton, with rope sandals. Their sombreros had extremely wide brims and were generally of straw.

In Ecuador, high-quality sombreros were made by plaiting the tough leaves of the toquilla palm, creating a fine, smooth, white finish. In 1855 an example of this type of hat was shown at the Paris Exhibition. Its popularity grew and the hat was issued to United States troops during the Spanish-American War of 1898. Later worn by engineers constructing the Panama Canal, it became known as the panama hat.

Indigenous Costume

The finest-quality clothing in Central and South America was made by indigenous peoples. Mayan women of Guatemala wove on backstrap looms (tensioned around the waist),

The Gauchos

The nineteenth century was the heyday of the gaucho, the cowboy of Argentina's Pampas grasslands. Gauchos were famous for physical toughness, a wild, swaggering lifestyle, and a strict code of honor. Many were mestizos (of mixed European and indigenous descent). The first gauchos wore their hair and mustaches long. Some wore caps or bandanas, while others wore hats with brims. White shirts and ponchos or scarlet cloaks were worn above wide pants. Leather boots with spurs and belts with heavy silver buckles completed the outfit.

producing colorful striped skirts, patterned belts, sashes, headgear, shawls, and square-cut blouses called *huipils.* The weavers of the Andes, such as the Aymara, wove fine ponchos and shawls (also used to carry babies) from camelid yarns such as alpaca.

In Chile, the Araucanian people wore long tunics and cloaks, while the natives of Patagonia wore blankets and skins. In the Amazon rainforest, many indigenous peoples wore no clothes at all, but patterned their bodies with vegetable dyes and pastes. Some wore clothes made of leaves or palm fronds, sometimes woven. Brilliant tropical feathers of the toucan or macaw were worn in headdresses.

The valleys of Patagonia are often cold and windswept. The native peoples, depicted in 1827, wear long, patterned blankets as warm cloaks.

In the 1850s, tunics and patterned poncho-style cloaks were being worn by the native Araucanian peoples of Chile, in the southern Andes.

Chapter 2: Europe: Nations and Costumes

Nineteenth-century Europe was a continent of great contrasts. Northern and western Europe, including Great Britain, France, and Germany, were at the center of an industrial revolution, with growing cities, new railroads, and factories. This was a time of rapid advances in technology and there was constant talk of progress. Southern and eastern Europe, however, remained largely rural. As a result, there was a yawning gap between the very rich and the very poor in Europe, which led to political strife and struggle.

In the 1850s, French fashion and manners were imitated by high society across Europe.

Much of Europe was still a patchwork of small states, which nationalists were trying forge into larger unions. Germany did not unite until 1871, the same year that modern Italy came into being. National rivalries within Europe created conflicts and wars throughout much of the century.

Class and Nation

All of these factors affected everyday costume. In cities such as Vienna, Berlin, London, Paris, and Rome, the rich would change clothes several times a day, parading in ball gowns or starched shirts and tailcoats, fashions which were admired and copied around the world. Dress was an indicator of subtle differences in social class—much more so than in the new cities of the United States. In Europe, a middle-class woman could not adopt the high fashions of the aristocracy without eyebrows being raised, while in New York City the wife of a successful merchant could dress pretty much as she pleased.

The growing middle class dressed conservatively and modestly. Europe's industrial workers wore plain working clothes and wooden-soled clogs. The men often wore flat caps. Many of the urban poor from the slums wore rags and their children went barefoot.

Country people were also often desperately poor. However, traditional costumes, with their embroidery, lace, or ribbons, were often still worn as everyday wear, as well as for festivals or special events. There was already a growing tendency among the middle and upper classes to consider these as "quaint" or "picturesque," or as romantic symbols of nationalism. The tartan plaid of the Scottish Highlanders was adopted by the British royal family at a time when the actual Highlanders were being evicted from their homes and leaving for a new life in Canada.

Nationalism was also behind the startling array of military costumes that soldiers wore on the battlefield.

Uniforms in bright scarlet, white, or blue, were adorned with braids, epaulettes and brass buttons. Khaki, the dull brown now used universally by soldiers, first appeared in the 1850s, but was not common until the 1890s.

New Technologies

New technologies in the textile industry were the driving forces behind the Industrial Revolution in the eighteenth and nineteenth centuries. Wool was no longer carded by hand but by giant wire-toothed cylinders. Water and then steam were used to power vast spinning machines called mules. In the cotton-weaving sheds, steam power drove clacking machine looms and great rollers. New chemical dyes such as mauveine and alizarin were produced in England and Germany.

This woman and man from Brittany in northern France wear national dress featuring a variety of fabrics – silk, satin, wool, velvet, and cotton.

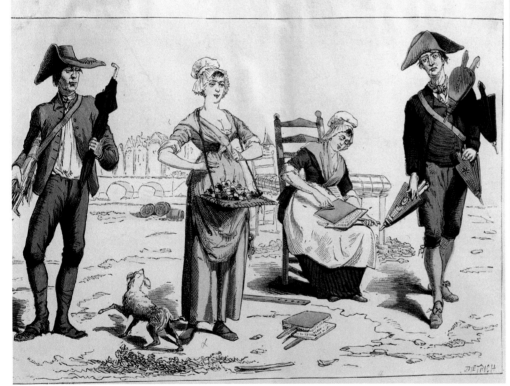

COSTUMES DE PARIS A TRAVERS LES SIÈCLES

An umbrella seller, a flower girl, a textile worker, and a bellows vendor illustrate working dress of the 1800s.

Paper Patterns

Making, sewing, and repairing clothes was standard work for housewives and maidservants. Paper dressmaking patterns, which were at first used only by professionals, were soon being distributed by women's magazines for amateur dressmakers. One of the first was *Dressmaking for Ladies – Universal Pattern Journal,* published in Dresden in 1844. By the 1880s and 1890s, paper patterns were highly popular and would remain so for another sixty years.

Western Europe

French Fashion

Formal evening dress is worn by all at this late-nineteenth-century social gathering.

Fashions of the early 1800s are shown in this picture of a milliner's (hat-maker's) workshop. Note the "empire line" dress.

Paris had dominated European fashion since the Middle Ages. Even the French revolutionaries of 1789 had hired designers to promote politically correct fashions featuring red, white, and blue, the colors that symbolized the new republic. In the 1790s and 1800s, French city fashions became increasingly exaggerated among the dandies or *incroyables* (incredibles). They wore shaggy haircuts and top hats, which were often pushed out of shape, a high stock wound around the neck right up to the chin, frock coats with extremely broad lapels, striped vests, and mid-calf boots with pointed toes.

Napoleon I, who became emperor in 1804, was determined to modernize the French textile industry. He imported new looms for mills at Sedan and Louviers and banned English textile imports. The northern French town of Valenciennes was famous for its lace and a fine satin called tulle. St. Quentin mills produced muslin and linen.

Napoleon I also sought the advice of the best tailors and fashion designers. An aristocratic French gentleman at this time might wear evening dress made up of a swallowtail coat, high-collared shirt and bow tie, and a silk-lined cape, with a top hat and cane.

Women were not allowed to present themselves at court wearing the same dress twice. Fashions such as the high-waisted chemise of the 1800s, known as the empire line, and the wide, bell-shaped crinoline of the 1850s, which were imitated all over the Western world, had their origins at the French court.

Charles Frederick Worth was an English fashion designer, born in Lincolnshire in 1825. At the age of twenty-one he moved to Paris and found work at Gagelin's fashion shop. He soon became a leader of taste and founded an establishment in the Rue de la Paix, that catered to the likes of Elizabeth, Empress of Austria, and Empress Eugénie de Montijo, the Spanish-born wife of Napoleon III of France. Eugénie was famed for her love of ribbons, frills, and lace.

Paris fashions of the later nineteenth century, such as the bustle and fishtail, were popular across Europe. In the 1890s, Paris became famous for its cafés, bars, and dance halls. Spangles and frills were worn by

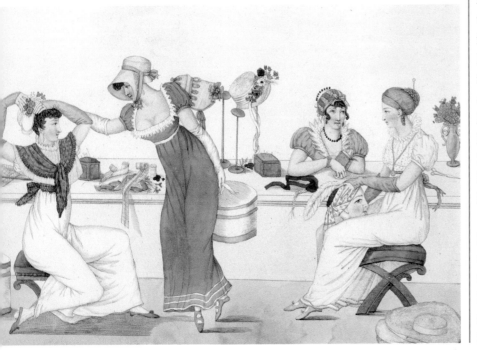

Fan Fashions

Folding fans were popular throughout Europe in the nineteenth century, especially in France, Spain, and Portugal. In the 1800s, small fans made of horn, bone, or ivory were popular. As dresses grew wider, so did the fans, many of which were made of lace or silk. Some were beautifully painted by hand, sometimes by the owner. China exported fans to Europe, but the most famous fan producer was a firm called La Maison Duvelleroy, which opened in Paris in 1827.

dancers and performers. The artists and down-at-heel poets who flocked to the city staged costume balls with shockingly daring outfits.

Although the provincial middle classes followed Paris fashion, in the coalfields of northern France, dress reflected only conditions of poverty and hardship. People wore heavy cotton and woolen working clothes and wooden clogs called sabots.

Many rural costumes were unique to the region. For example, in the northwest of France, Breton women wore towering headdresses (coiffes) of white lace and ribbons at festivals, markets, and church services, while their husbands wore black hats with a wide, up-curved brim.

Southern Europe

Spain

Veils and shawls had been an important part of Spanish women's dress since before the Middle Ages, and the veiled headdress, or mantilla, became established in the sixteenth century. By the early nineteenth century, this had become a statement of high fashion rather than a regional costume, and it was adopted in the 1840s and 1850s by Queen Isabella II. The nineteenth-century mantilla was made of lace–black for Holy Week and white for celebrations such as bullfights or Seville's spring festival and fashion parade, the Feria. It was secured by a high comb of tortoiseshell.

Spanish urban men's dress generally mirrored that of the European capitals of the day. Cloaks and capes were popular, as were short riding jackets and fine leather boots for horsemen. The Spanish love of festival costume found its expression in the ornate dress of the bullfighters, which included short jackets of satin embroidered in gold and silver thread, breeches, stockings, and slippers without heels. This style is still worn today.

Villagers dance in the open air in an Italian village.

Italy, Greece, and the Balkans

For most of the nineteenth century, Italy was a patchwork of states in the process of forging itself into a single nation. The Balkan region was divided between the Austro-Hungarian Empire and the Ottoman Empire of the Turks. Between 1814 and 1832, the Greeks struggled for independence from Turkish rule. The dress of the Greek mountain fighters – a tasseled cap, short kilt, and woolen leggings – became the national costume of the new country and is still worn by Greece's national guard, the *Evzónes*.

In cities such as Milan, Rome, and Naples, Western dress was common to all classes. Many wealthy northern Europeans visited Italy, and the Lido at Venice became the most fashionable resort in Europe – a seaside parade of the latest styles in dresses, hats, and parasols.

Folk Costume

The nineteenth century was a high point in the production of homemade folk costumes in southern Europe. The sheer variety of folk costumes was enormous. On the island of Sardinia, there were hundreds of types of costume. Every town and village had its own style of veil, lace, and embroidery.

Folk costumes were brought out for harvest festivals, religious processions,

Camicie Rosse

Giuseppe Garibaldi (1807–1882) fought for a free, united Italy and became a national hero. He also fought in South America. Garibaldi and his followers were known as the *Camicie Rosse*, or Red Shirts, for the color of the shirts they wore. Some believe the shirts were purchased as a job lot in Montevideo, South America, and had originally been intended for slaughterhouse workers. Others say that Garibaldi got the idea of the red shirts from New York City, where he lived from about 1850 to 1853. Red flannel shirts were worn by companies of volunteer firefighters in that city.

In 1860, one thousand Red Shirt volunteers set sail from Genoa to assist rebels against the Bourbon dynasty on the island of Sicily, and then crossed to the mainland and won territory for Victor Emmanuel II. A simple item of clothing became famous around the world as the symbol of a political movement.

and weddings. Dresses would be handed down from mother to daughter and form part of the bridal trousseau. In the Dolomite region of northeastern Italy, men would give silver or gold vest chains to their godsons as a token of their coming of age. Bangles or rings were brought back by migrant workers or sailors for their loved ones, and these became status symbols in the home community.

In some regions, plainer versions of folk costumes were worn as everyday clothing. This was the case on the Greek island of Crete, where common male dress in mountain villages was a vest, baggy trousers with a broad sash, knee-length boots, a cape over one shoulder, and a black fringed headscarf.

Folk costume did not just indicate the location of a village, but also gave clues about the wearer's social status. Wealth might be indicated by the quality and dye of the cloth, by the number of buttons, or by the type of metal used for rings worn on fingers. Marital status might be signaled by the color of dress or type of hairstyle, or by the color of a man's vest. Widowhood was often indicated by the wearing of black, although green was worn in parts of Sardinia. Folk costume played an important part in courting, too. For example, a girl might give one of her apron ribbons to a suitor as a token of her favor.

Male (above) and female costume (far left) from the southern Balkans.

Northern Europe

North Sea Coasts

Across Norway, Sweden, and Denmark, folk costume varied from one district to the next and often included long dresses with embroidered bodices worn over blouses, as well as aprons and headdresses.

Frisian and Dutch traditional dress also included many regional variations. Dutch men might wear very wide trousers and peaked caps. Dutch women wore full skirts and a wide variety of lace caps. Wooden clogs were common among farmers and market traders. Belgium, which broke away from the Netherlands to become an independent country in 1830, was famous for its long-established tradition of lace-making, which reached its height in this century.

German *Tracht*

The German word for folk costume is *Tracht*. The styles worn in Bavaria, German-speaking Switzerland, and Austria in the nineteenth century started as the working dress of country people such as foresters and dairy maids, varying considerably according to district and profession. More elaborate costumes were worn for festival days, such as the *Bollenhut*, still worn in the Gutach district of the Black Forest in southwestern Germany. Worn over a silk cap, this was a straw hat decorated with fourteen woolen pom-poms—red for unmarried women and black for married women.

By the 1870s, *Tracht* had become associated with idealized, romantic notions of country life, and the middle and upper classes began

A grenadier guard from Baden, in the uniform of 1806, dresses to impress. Baden was a duchy in Germany which, from 1805, supported France in the Napoleonic wars.

Arctic Europe

In the nineteenth century, the Saami people, or Lapps, who inhabited the far north of Scandinavia, lived principally by herding reindeer. They used reindeer skin to make boots with upturned toes, tied at the ankle with woolen garters. The boots were stuffed with hay for insulation. Saami tunics were made of red and blue woolen cloth, decorated with colorful braids, tassels, and ribbons. Cloth was produced on upright looms in which the warp threads were tensioned by weights.

adopting it as dress for leisure time, hunting, and even formal occasions. Lederhosen (leather knee-length breeches), woolen socks, and feathered felt hats were worn by men. For women, the tightly bodiced dirndl, or *Gewand*, was a dress with a full skirt and an apron of a contrasting color, often worn sleeveless over a lacy or embroidered blouse.

Fashionable Society

In the 1890s, smart society glittered at the spa resort of Baden-Baden, or at the Zoological Gardens in Berlin. The northeastern tradition of Prussia was austere and conservative, and military uniforms were much in evidence. The Kaiser (emperor) himself appeared in public in the spiked helmet, or *Pickelhaube*, of the army.

Vienna, capital of Austria-Hungary and home of the waltz, was a city famed for its gaiety throughout the nineteenth century. Elegant fashions were to be seen at court, on the Ringstrasse, in the restaurants, theaters, and ballrooms.

This 1898 painting by the Viennese artist Gustav Klimt shows the shimmering, gauzy dress of Sonja Knipps, the wife of a wealthy industrialist.

Central and Eastern Europe

This young woman wears the traditional bodice and blouse of the Tatra mountain region, on the border between Poland and Slovakia.

During the nineteenth century, most of central Europe—the territory of the Baltic peoples, the Poles, Czechs, Slovaks, Hungarians, Romanians, and Bulgarians—was governed by other countries, including Germany, Russia, Austria-Hungary, and the Ottoman Empire of the Turks. The region had rich traditions of folk costume, and many people wore these as a means of asserting their cultural identity and desire for nationhood.

Some central and eastern European costumes were influenced by Asian traditions. In Poland, for example—an area of Asian incursion in the Middle Ages—the traditional men's festival dress was said to derive from the Middle East. It included red and white striped trousers, a long blue vest, and a hat trimmed with lambskin and peacock feathers.

Bohemians, Poles, and Hungarians

In the early nineteenth century, peasant women in Bohemia (part of the modern Czech Republic) would still wear linen spun by hand from home-grown flax. This was made into blouses, aprons, and skirts for everyday wear. The finest linen was reserved for clothes worn on festivals such as May Day.

In the Lowicz region of Poland, men's festival costume included white linen shirts with embroidered collars, colorful striped trousers in high black boots, black jackets, and black felt hats. Women's festival costume included wide-sleeved embroidered

Yarmulke and *Streimel*

Central and eastern Europe had a large Jewish population in the nineteenth century. Men kept their heads covered as a mark of respect for God, generally with a skullcap or *yarmulke*. Some Hasidic Jews (members of a religious movement that grew up in Poland in the eighteenth century) wore a round hat called a *streimel*, trimmed with sable fur. Long side curls *(payos)* and beards belonged to a more ancient Jewish tradition.

blouses, black bodices decorated with beadwork, and full striped skirts.

The Podhale costume of the northern slopes of Poland's Tatra mountains is still worn today. Men wear tight-fitting trousers of white homespun wool decorated with embroidery, leather slippers, buckled belts, brimmed felt hats with an eagle feather and hat band of shells, and a heavy cape. Women wear red, blue, or green skirts with floral designs, frilled blouses, and embroidered velvet vests, tied by a ribbon.

Hungarian costumes show some of the finest embroidery in this region, as well as leather and felt appliqué, and decorative tassels, braids, and pom-poms.

The Russians

In European Russia, the imperial court wore elegant dress in the style of Paris. The urban middle classes also wore the styles of western Europe. Peaked caps were commonly worn by men of all classes from the 1880s onward.

In the countryside, the poverty-stricken peasants wore, as everyday dress, linen tunics to the thigh or knee, belts or sashes, long overcoats, and high boots or tied leg-bindings. Tunic and boots were also worn informally by other classes as a kind of Russian national costume. Hair was often worn long, with a full beard. Women wore long skirts with blouses, aprons, headscarves, and shawls.

Appliqué work decorates the cloak of a Hungarian man.

Special dress for religious festivals or weddings included various headdresses, full skirts with banded decorations, and lace. Decorative borders were often added with a technique called needle-weaving, whereby threads at the edges of the textile were cut, drawn, stitched, and interwoven with colored yarn.

Cossack men of the steppe grasslands of southern Russia and the Ukraine wore tunics sewn with cartridge holders for their guns. They also wore high boots and long sheepskin coats with tall, shaggy hats of sheep's wool. Cossack troops fought against the French emperor Napoleon's invading army in 1812 and formed a royal bodyguard for the Russian *czars* (emperors).

Russia had a rich variety of folk costumes.

Chapter 3: Western Dress: at Work and Play

In medieval Europe, uniforms had been rare, except for the habits of monastic orders or the liveries worn by the servants or retainers of feudal lords. The first true military uniforms did not appear in Europe until the seventeenth century. These reached a highly decorative point at the time of the Napoleonic wars. After that, as weapon technology advanced and warfare modernized, uniforms became more practical.

The Chef's *Toque*

France was not just the center of nineteenth-century fashion, but also of fine cooking, or haute cuisine. Cooks had long worn hats to keep their hair out of the way, but it was in the 1800s that the modern chef's "uniform" first became popular.

One man who had great influence in the world's kitchens was Parisian chef Marie-Antoine Carême (1784–1833), who wrote *La Cuisine Française (French Cooking)* in 1828. He had his cooks dress in double-breasted jackets of starched white cotton, because they looked clean, fresh, and smart, and because the material was easily washable. A cotton cloth or neckerchief was worn around the neck to mop the brow in the heat of the kitchen.

The lower orders of chef wore caps of white cotton, but head chefs were expected to wear a tall, cylindrical hat of white cotton, the *toque blanche*. Carême's own *toque* is said to have been eighteen inches (45 cm) high. Legend says that the first toques were made with a hundred pleats to show that a good chef could cook an egg in a hundred different ways! The French chef's uniform was soon being worn in hotels around the world.

The nineteenth century witnessed the establishment of many public institutions, including police forces, fire services, and hospitals, and each of these institutions adopted uniforms for their employees. Such uniforms boosted the status of public servants and gave them pride in their jobs. It also made them easy for the public to identify in the event of trouble or an emergency.

Looking Back

Many traditional costumes continued much the same as they had done in previous centuries among the more conservative sections of society. Religious dress remained based on archaic styles of clothing. Monarchs were still crowned in medieval robes, even if they did wear modern dress or uniforms at other times. In many countries, nobles also wore fur-trimmed robes or other emblems of rank dating back to the Middle Ages for ceremonial occasions.

Menservants employed by the nobility often wore liveried uniforms in the eighteenth-century style, with breeches and stockings. The men's curled wigs, long abandoned by the general public, continued to be worn by sections of the clergy and legal profession in Britain and some British colonies, as a badge of office.

Fashions for the Future

Many types of dress which in the nineteenth century were regarded as work clothes or sporting outfits, became everyday dress for all classes

in the twentieth century. For example, knitted sweaters were chiefly worn by fishermen from the North and Irish Sea coasts in the nineteenth century. The pattern of the knit revealed the fisherman's home port. Famous examples included the Aran (from the Irish Aran Islands) and the Guernsey and Jersey (from the Channel Islands). Jersey became a name for any type of warm top or for knitwear in general.

Wool contains lanolin, a natural grease which resists water, so it was the ideal material for fishermen's sweaters. They were first worn in Norway and around the British Isles.

Clerics and Clerks

Priests

The vestments of priests are the clothes worn during worship, such as the surplice, stole, cope, alb, and chasuble. These began as the secular dress of the early Christian era. Then, during the Middle Ages, vestments gradually acquired symbolic significance, often reflecting differences in teaching and customs between the various Christian Churches. In Europe and the Americas in the nineteenth century, these details were still held to be matters of the greatest importance.

At one extreme of religious dress were the rich gold vestments and robes of the Eastern Orthodox Church, and at the other the simple black "Geneva gown" of the Calvinist tradition. In the Anglican Church, dress was at the center of a bitter controversy in the 1870s between "Anglo-Catholics" and more Protestant factions. The former enjoyed ritual and placed great emphasis on colorful, embroidered vestments. The latter, in contrast, called for greater simplicity, and preferred to dress in plain cassocks and surplices.

The everyday dress of the clergy was also a matter of great importance at a time when the Church was a dominant influence in everyday life. Ecclesiastical dress identified the social role of its wearer and his rank in the Church hierarchy, from the black soutane, or cassock, of a Catholic priest, to the buttoned gaiters worn by Anglican bishops.

Nineteenth-century ecclesiastical dress, such as the chasuble on the right, remained medieval in design.

Students

The academic dress of the English universities of Oxford and Cambridge was widely copied in North America, in the British Empire, and other parts of the English-speaking world. It was comprised of a black undergraduate gown and various other full-sleeved gowns, the design of which dated back to the Middle Ages. A silk or fur hood, rather like a monk's cowl, was worn folded over the shoulders. The Oxford academic cap, called a "square," was nicknamed a "mortarboard" in the 1850s, because its shape resembled that of the board on which builders mixed mortar.

Other European countries had their own traditions of academic dress, including frock coats, gowns, and caps of linen or silk. In Germany, the sword-dueling fraternities known as the *Burschenschaften* reached the height of their popularity. These groups of aristocratic students, at universities such as Heidelberg, wore elaborate uniforms with peaked or pillbox hats, and proudly displayed on their cheeks the scars of their battles.

Judges and Lawyers

Judicial costume had its origins in ecclesiastical and academic dress. English lawyers, like ministers of religion, wore a collar with two descending strips of cloth, called bands. In many countries, judges and lawyers wore black gowns or caps, but the English judges' robes of silk and fur, and the full horsehair wig in the style of the 1680s, were probably the strangest costumes to be seen in nineteenth-century European courts. The new nation of the United States was quick to abandon this particular English tradition. By the 1860s, English lawyers were being allowed to remove their wigs on hot days, and some wondered whether the wearing of wigs might be abandoned altogether. However, the wearing of wigs continues in law courts in England—and in much of Canada— to this day.

Weddings and Funerals

The dress of the church congregation was also very formal in the nineteenth century, with women covering their heads with a veil or hat. In many parts of Europe, church weddings were an opportunity to wear traditional folk costume. In northern Europe, best clothes were worn for weddings, but there was no standard bridal costume as there is today. Extravagant black costume was worn by both men and women at nineteenth-century funerals and over long periods of mourning.

A French couple enjoy a wedding feast in 1886. Best clothes were worn, but the conventions of dress for a wedding were not strict.

Public Uniforms

At the start of the nineteenth century, public order in most European countries was the responsibility of army units, civil militias, or watchmen, and their treatment of offenders was generally either brutal or else ineffective. The growing cities of the industrial age required a new form of policing.

Peelers and Coppers

The first modern police force was established in England in 1829 by Sir Robert Peel. The first "Peelers," as the police officers were known, wore a distinctive blue uniform. London became the model for many new police forces around the world, such as that in New York City, where a copper star on the Peeler-style uniform gave the force their nickname, the "coppers." Blue became a common police uniform color in many countries.

In the same year that uniformed police started walking the streets of London, "sergeants" were introduced in Paris, the first French police force to wear a uniform. They carried swords and were dressed somewhat archaically in cocked hats. They were later also recruited in other cities such as Lyon. Not until 1870, when they were renamed Peacekeepers, did they adopt the famous *képi,* a cylindrical peaked cap.

Towards the end of the century, variants of the German spiked helmet, the *Pickelhaube,* were adopted by many European and colonial police forces. The French resisted this trend, however, perhaps because the design remained associated with the German invasion of their country during the Franco-Prussian war of 1870–71.

Helmets and Axes

Before the nineteenth century, firefighters had been employed by private companies, insurance firms, or by volunteer groups. Some wore private liveries. As public fire brigades with horse-drawn carriages became common in the nineteenth century, firefighters across the Western world became public heroes, adorned in smart uniforms and brass or leather helmets, and wielding ornate fire axes.

Nursing Dress

In many Catholic countries, hospital nursing remained the job of nuns, who still wore long dresses, wimples, and linen veils or headdresses, in a style which had changed little since the Middle Ages. When proper medical training was first given to nurses—for example at the Nightingale School of Nursing, founded at St Thomas's Hospital in London in 1860—new nursing costumes remained true to traditional styles. The uniform included long dresses, starched white aprons (often hung with useful items such as scissors or keys), and lace headdresses or short veils.

Prison Uniforms

Uniforms for police, firemen, and nurses were designed to give status to public servants. By contrast, nineteenth-century prisoners were issued with uniforms in order to take away their individuality and self-respect. Prison uniforms were drab in color and made from cotton or coarse cloth. They were often made distinctive, with stripes for example, so that escaped prisoners could more easily be recaptured. Government-issue prison clothing in Britain and its colonies was marked with a broad arrow print.

Charity Dress

Charitable organizations also favored uniform dress in the nineteenth century as a visible sign of their good works. For example, in many countries, such as the Netherlands, orphans were dressed in distinctive

This painting of 1886 shows a Russian nurse. The nun-like costume and cross derive from the medieval tradition of nursing.

uniforms. Many orphanages in Europe dressed their children in particular colors or styles, and elderly people who relied on communal support in grim workhouses, or in poorhouses, might also be required to wear a uniform.

Housemaids

In the late nineteenth century, even middle-class families in Europe and North America employed nannies, cooks, and housemaids. The latter were expected to wear a uniform, most often a black dress and a white apron, with a lace cap or bonnet.

Sports and Leisure

At the Seaside
Visiting the seaside for pleasure became fashionable at the start of the nineteenth century, and as railroads linked cities to the coast, all classes began to enjoy days on the beach, shrimping and donkey riding. At first, visitors wore full crinolines, bonnets, and city suits. As sea bathing became more and more popular, people gradually became less modest. Taken to the water in horse-drawn, wheeled huts called bathing machines, women would put on skirted bathing costumes and caps with frills and bows before descending into the waves. Men would wear long woolen bathing costumes, covering the torso and upper legs.

Organized sports became a passion for many during the nineteenth century, particularly among the upper classes. Gymnastics were popular, and all kinds of team games and ball games were given formal rules. Inspired by the athletic ideals of the classical world, the Olympic Games were reinvented in Athens in 1896—the first time they had been staged since 393 CE.

The love of sport may have started in upper-class schools and universities, but by the 1890s it had spread to bank clerks and factory workers. Sporting activities had a great influence on how people dressed in the Western world, for they demanded informal, less constricting dress.

Team Colors
Sports which became popular in Europe and North America in the nineteenth century included rowing, tennis, various forms of football, lacrosse, field hockey, cricket, and baseball. The players of the nineteenth century were mainly amateurs, and sporting dress was still very individual and not in any way streamlined for action or speed. Breeches were often still worn rather than shorts.

Bold patterns such as stripes, hoops, quarters, or diamonds helped to distinguish teams on muddy fields, just as heraldic patterns had identified knights on the medieval battlefield. Teams were also indicated by badges, tasseled or peaked caps, sweaters, and by colorful braided or striped jackets, known as blazers.

The standard modern dress for jockeys evolved in the nineteenth century, although riders in horse races had worn team colors since classical times.

Racing Silk

Horse racing remained popular in Europe throughout the nineteenth century. Jockeys wore an outfit very much like that of riders today, with riding boots and breeches, peaked caps and brightly colored silk liveries to identify the racehorse's owner. This was one sporting event where the crowd did not dress casually. The great races were a chance for the aristocracy to show off the latest dresses, hats, and parasols. However, all social classes attended the races and wore their fanciest outfits.

Boating

Boating became increasingly popular in North America and Europe in the late nineteenth century. University students took part in rowing races as a sport, wearing athletic jerseys for sculling, and blazers and sweaters when off the river. Boating was also popular as a leisure pastime, and the "boater," a hard, flat straw hat with a brim and a colorful hatband, often in sporting team colors, was soon being worn as part of everyday wear.

Women Outdoors

Cycling clubs were very popular from the 1880s onward. Male cyclists often wore breeches and peaked caps, but some female cyclists caused a stir by wearing outfits with knee-length baggy pants, showing their stockinged legs. A French fashion plate of the period shows a woman in a country shooting party wearing a suit with a knee-length skirt over breeches and knee-high gaiters. Lawn tennis was popular at this time, but it was still played by men in long flannel trousers and by women in long dresses and aprons and even large floral hats.

Two ladies in baggy pants ride a tandem, or "bicycle-built-for-two." Such costumes shocked the older generation.

The Entertainers

The French painter Edgar Degas captures the costume and excitement of a performance in Paris in 1876.

Stage dress played an important part in the history of costume in the nineteenth century. Actors generally performed dramas in conventional costume with greasepainted faces before flickering footlights, but there were many other forms of costumed entertainment.

Tutus and Garlands

Many ballets were inspired by folk dances, and dancers would wear appropriate regional costume. This innovation was championed above all by the Austrian-born ballerina Fanny Elssler in the 1830s. Appearing in Europe, North America, and Russia, she would wear costume in an Italian style to dance the tarantella, in Spanish style to dance the cachucha, and in Polish style to dance the Cracovienne. Such costumed "character" dances became an enduring feature of romantic ballets.

The romantic style of ballet was popularized by the dancer Marie Taglioni in *La Sylphide* (1832). Female ballet costumes of this style were often worn with a sash tied behind in a bow. They had shorter, generally knee- to mid-calf-length hems, in marked contrast to everyday dress, which covered the legs completely. The flared, gauzy tutu had an ethereal look, well suited to magical tales of fairies and spirits, as were the garlands and scarves which often played a part in the choreography. The ribbon-laced satin ballet pump dates from this period, enabling nimble footwork. Blocked toes were added for dancing *sur les pointes* (on tiptoe). During the Romantic period of the ballet, which lasted until the 1870s, it was common for women also to play men's roles, wearing male dress.

Music Hall and the Cancan

More down-to-earth entertainment could be found at the popular variety shows, known as music hall, burlesque, or vaudeville. These shows launched many personalities who were as famous as the pop or movie stars of today. Female singers and dancers of the 1880s and 1890s wore decorative dresses with skirts only to the knee, at a time when most women revealed no more than an ankle. On these stages, too, it was common for women to impersonate men in their acts.

Late nineteenth-century Parisian performers knew how to shock polite society. The French capital was renowned for wild, noisy dances such as the cancan, in which high leg-kicks showed off lacy underwear. The artists and poets who flocked to the city liked to flaunt their extravagant and eccentric dress at costumed balls.

Audiences

While the lower-class throng at a music hall or circus wore everyday dress, the wealthy audiences at city theaters, opera houses, and concert halls wore formal evening dress and formed a spectacle in their own right. The wealthiest sat in the side "boxes" to be admired by all. The women put on their finest dresses,

By the time Degas painted *The Dance Class* in about 1874, romantic costume had become the standard for ballet dancers.

their diamond necklaces, earrings, and glittering tiaras, and wore capes or cloaks.

The men wore tailcoats, vests, starched shirts, and stiff collars. From the early nineteenth century onward, men wore an "opera cloak" to the theater rather than the everyday greatcoat. The cloak was black, made of wool or velvet, lined with colored silk, and fastened with silk cords. Until about 1840, men wore a cocked hat or bicorne for a visit to the opera. However this was generally superseded by the "opera hat," a collapsible silk top hat, patented in 1837.

Circus and Pantomime

The harlequinade of the eighteenth century was a mime show of characters wearing stock costumes, such as the white-faced Pierrot. The harlequinade influenced popular theater and evolved into circus clowning. Clowns developed a whole range of costumes and characters in the nineteenth century, with grotesque makeup, baggy pants, corkscrew hair, tall hats, pom-poms, false noses, and outsized shoes.

By the end of the nineteenth century, the circus was hugely popular across Europe and North America. Performers wore very different costumes from their modestly dressed audiences. Female trapeze artists, jugglers, tightrope walkers, and bareback horse riders wore knee-length dresses or spangled leotards that revealed the whole thigh, with ankle-length boots.

Children's Dress

Before the nineteenth century, children's dress in Western countries had largely consisted of scaled-down versions of adult dress. For many children, this remained the case in the 1800s. After all, many poor children did adult jobs, working in mines or cotton mills. In city slums, boys and girls wore rags and secondhand clothes. Many went barefoot.

However, in middle- and upper-class homes, children now began to be recognized, rather sentimentally, as a class of people deserving their own forms of dress. Children had no say themselves in what clothes they wore, and their outfits were often uncomfortable. Children's clothing was always the decision of the mother.

A child from a well-off home would first be presented to the world in a lace christening robe, often beautifully made and passed down from one generation to the next. For the first years of childhood, there was little difference between dress for boys and girls. Both sexes wore dresses over pantalettes (long, lacy pants), and buttoned boots to the lower calf.

Boys' Dress

Between the ages of three and six, boys would be "breeched," or put into breeches, which were often worn below a pleated tunic. From the mid-nineteenth century onward, boy's fashions included various standard styles which remained popular for decades.

Sailor suits

One boy's fashion was the sailor suit, which was popular across the Western world. Made in blue serge or white cotton, it featured a jacket or shirt with a striped blue-and-white collar. This formed a flap over the shoulders at the back and was knotted below the lapels, in imitation of naval uniforms. It was often worn with a sailor hat, a flat-brimmed straw hat with a low crown and a black ribbon. Girls and young women also adopted the sailor-suit collar and hat.

For example, caps in various military styles were popular in many countries. In Britain, the royal family popularized the wearing of "Scotch" kilts and "glengarry" caps among boys, and variants of this style soon spread overseas. Knickerbockers were breeches of tweed or other cloth buttoned below the knee and worn with a collarless jacket. Later, the trousers hung loose at the knee, without buttoning. Older boys would wear long pants. Fishermen's woolen sweaters became popular with boys towards the end of the century, especially at the seaside.

Girls' Dress

In the first half of the nineteenth century, girl's costume remained much the same as that of adult women, from the early high-waisted dresses to the later fuller-skirted designs, often worn above pantalettes. Hems were shorter than those of adult dresses.

Simpler dresses worn in the 1860s must have allowed girls to lead a more active life, and were often worn with a cotton pinafore on top and a flannel petticoat and drawers beneath. Long stockings of black wool or white cotton were commonly worn.

The bonnets of the early century were replaced by round-brimmed felt hats, straw hats, or woolen tam-o'-shanters—caps of Scottish origin with a flat crown larger than the headband, and often a pom-pom.

Tell Tale Tit,
Your tongue shall be slit;
And all the dogs in the town
Shall have a little bit.

This nursery rhyme book was illustrated by Kate Greenaway (1846–1901). Her work shows a variety of children's dress in the nineteenth century.

Chapter 4: Empires and Colonies

In the nineteenth century, much of the Americas broke away from European rule. At the same time, vast areas of Africa, Asia, and Oceania became part of new overseas European empires, or at least fell under their influence. The chief imperial powers were Britain, France, the Netherlands, Belgium, Germany (after 1871), Portugal, and Spain.

Other major nineteenth-century empires – those of Austria, Russia, China, and the Ottoman Turks – were essentially expansions outward from their home territories. The United States also acquired some overseas territories. It did not build up a large empire, but it did intervene in the affairs of China and Japan to advance its trade.

In some lands, such as Australia and New Zealand, southern Africa, and India, the Europeans settled and made permanent homes. In others, they came only to conquer and govern, to control trade and take resources. The Europeans who moved to these often remote parts of the world included explorers, soldiers, administrators, missionaries, teachers, business people, farmers, planters, and miners.

Indigenous peoples were often treated harshly and their land was taken from them. Many of the imperialists were racists who believed that Europeans were superior to other peoples. Despite these attitudes, some of the European newcomers began to adopt items of local dress, and the words used for them sometimes entered the language of the colonial power. For example, the Urdu word *payejama* (leg coverings), meaning the loose cotton or silk trousers common in the Punjab region of India, was adopted in English as *pajamas* by 1800.

At the same time, local people adopted items of European dress, especially those who worked for the new colonial masters, such as officials or soldiers. Trousers, frock coats,

Two cultures met in nineteenth-century India. The bearded Indian man wears a turban and loose tunic, while the British man wears typical European dress and riding boots.

In 1871, two famous explorers met in East Africa. H. M. Stanley is shown here in *sola topi* and *puggarree*, while David Livingstone wears his favorite peaked cap.

shirts, and long cotton dresses all began to be worn. This was often at the insistence of Christian missionaries who believed that traditional costume, which was often more revealing than Western dress, was in some way sinful and inferior to European attire.

Even traditional dress began to be made from imported cloth. Cotton might by grown in India, exported to a textile mill in Manchester, England, and then exported as cloth back to the country which had produced it in the first place. The colonies provided not just raw materials, but new markets for European products.

Pith Helmets

One item of clothing above all others came to symbolize the age of empire—the *sola topi* (also known as a topee or pith helmet). *Topi* was the word for hat in the Hindi language, and *sola* was the plant whose stem provided a fibrous pith used in the manufacture of this item. The sola topi was a curved lightweight helmet which protected the forehead, crown, and neck from the tropical sun. A scarf called a *puggarree* was sometimes wrapped around it as a kind of hatband. The helmet, generally colored white or khaki, originated in India. It was chiefly worn by the Europeans, both male and female—by explorers, missionaries, soldiers, and traders from Africa to Southeast Asia. In some places it was adopted by native officials and other local people, and it can still be seen in parts of Southeast Asia.

African Dress

In the nineteenth century, African traditional dress could still be seen in its finest and most elaborate forms, but at the same time traded manufactured cloths and beads were beginning to affect indigenous fashions. Colonial outfits included military uniforms and official dress, as well as the clothing worn by settlers, farmers, and pioneers–typically a

A variety of uniforms was worn by the French Foreign Legion in France's overseas colonies. Note the neck cloth attached to the *képi*.

broad-brimmed hat and knee-length boots with a jacket, tough trousers, and a cotton or linen shirt.

Colonial Uniforms

African colonial troops of the nineteenth century wore a great variety of uniforms. Some of these were based on native African styles. For example, the *zouave* uniform, adopted by some French and even United States regiments in the 1850s, had its origins in the dress of the Zouave tribe of the Kabyle Berbers of North Africa. It included the *chéchia* (a tasseled cap), a vest, voluminous baggy pants, and gaiters.

Perhaps the most famous colonial uniform was that of the mercenaries who joined the French Foreign Legion, founded in 1831. The soldiers dressed in blue tailcoats, red trousers, and the cylindrical peaked cap or *képi*, which could be worn with a flap at the back as protection against the sun.

The Fez

Cotton robes in the Arab style were worn across North and Saharan Africa, with European dress also beginning to make an appearance in cities. Also popular here was the fez, a hat named after the city of Fez in Morocco, where it was originally made. The fez looked like an up-ended flowerpot and was made of red-dyed felt with a black tassel. The fez was adopted as a uniform hat by many native troops in colonial service in East and West Africa. Morocco was also famous for its silk sashes, slippers, coarse woolen cloaks, and soft tooled leather.

Zulu Battledress

The weapons of the African warriors who fought against colonial invaders were no match for modern firearms. One of the few peoples to inflict a defeat on the British were the Zulus of southern Africa, in 1879. The Zulus fought principally with stabbing spears, clubs called knobkerries, and with shields. They wore breechclouts of calfskin with the fur of monkey, civet, or genet hanging like tails in the front.

Headgear included: simple ring circlets made of fiber, gum, and wax; headbands of leopard or otter fur; earflaps of monkey fur; or more elaborate headdresses, including ostrich plumes, long feathers, porcupine quills, or sometimes cow horns, depending on rank. Arm- and leg-fringes were made of cows' tails. Brass armbands and necklaces of wooden beads were awarded to warriors for acts of bravery.

A Zulu warrior of 1849 is shown in full battledress, which was intended to strike fear into his enemy.

The First *Kangas*

One of the most common items of dress worn by women in East Africa today is the *kanga*, a brightly printed cotton wrap. This style of dress originated among the Swahili women of Zanzibar in the 1850s. Instead of buying cotton cloth in small sections, suitable for kerchiefs, as they had previously, the women began to double up the lengths or to sew kerchief sections together. These now formed large, decorative cloths which were wound around the body. Today's cloths have bold border patterns featuring written Swahili proverbs, but the first ones are believed to have been spotted—for the word *kanga* means "guinea fowl," known for its speckled plumage.

The finest African cloth was produced in West Africa on horizontal treadle looms, following a tradition dating back to the Middle Ages. The hand-woven cloth (*nsaduaso* or *nwontoma*) of the Asanti people of Ghana was of the highest quality. Most famous was their *kente* (basket-weave) cloth, in which strips of woven textile were sewn together. Kente cloth was worn for important festivals and ceremonies. Beautiful gold jewelry and regalia have also survived from many regions of nineteenth-century West Africa.

Masks and Adornments

Across sub-Saharan Africa there was a vast range of clothing and adornment materials, including wild animal hides and furs, cow hide, the barkcloth of the Baganda people, grasses and leaves, cotton, and feathers. Bodies and faces were patterned or plastered with ocher, ash (sometimes used as an insect repellant), or dyes. Teeth were sometimes filed to a point, or skin might be cut to create a pattern of scars representing tribal or clan loyalties.

Among the Niger-Congo family of peoples, masks were very important, and were used in battle, in dances, in ceremonies, and in rites such as funerals. Some were designed to be terrifying or beautiful, and others to look like animals. They were made of wood, brass, feathers, shells, fur, fibers, and paint.

The Ottoman Empire of the Turks stretched from the Balkan peninsula of southeastern Europe, southward into Syria, Iraq, Palestine, and Arabia, and eastward across modern Turkey. The empire was in decline from the eighteenth century onward, and in the nineteenth century it lost important territories such as Greece.

Turkey was famous for its fine textiles, and the Turks produced many traditional coated costumes made of striped satin, a combination of silk and cotton which was often striped red

A nineteenth-century studio photographer records female costume from Turkey (left) and the Arabian peninsula (right). Both regions were part of the Ottoman empire.

and yellow. The wearing of luxurious cloth next to the skin was discouraged by Islamic dress codes, but the weave of the satin gave the cloth a silk surface, while leaving plain cotton on the inside.

Sultan Selim III, who died in 1808, was the last Turkish ruler to wear the traditional large turban and robes. His successor, Mahmud II, adopted trousers and a cape, and made the red fez the official male headwear of the Ottoman Empire, worn by officials and the public instead of turbans. Baggy trousers, sashes, and vests were commonly worn by Turkish men.

In the Arab lands controlled by the Ottoman Turks, traditional dress remained as it was since the Middle Ages, suited to the hot climate and Muslim dress codes which emphasized modesty. Men wore a full cotton robe, known as the *aba*, and a long head covering secured by a black headband, the *agal*. Women wore ankle-length dresses and, in most regions, a veil.

Traditional everyday male costume worn in Persia (modern Iran) during the Qajar dynasty.

Persian Dancers

Many ancient Persian (Iranian) dance traditions were lost over the ages because of foreign invasion and Muslim codes of modesty. However, dance did thrive at the royal court in the nineteenth century, when Persia was ruled by the Qajar dynasty. The professional female dancers were sumptuously attired in colorful, intricately patterned costumes. Fabrics were embroidered with gold thread and decorated with pearls and gems. Dancers generally wore a long skirt over trousers, a blouse, and a long-sleeved jacket which flared out over the hips. Pearl necklaces and jeweled armlets were popular with the dancers, who also wore a small hat topped by a feather. Hair was worn long.

The Raj in India

At the start of the nineteenth century, India was effectively governed by a commercial organization, the British East India Company. Following an uprising in 1857, known as the Indian Mutiny, British government rule was imposed. British India was known as the Raj, and its territories included modern-day Pakistan and Bangladesh, neighboring Burma (modern-day Myanmar), and Ceylon (Sri Lanka).

Cottons and Silks

India was a major center of world cotton and silk production. Across this vast region a great array of traditional costume continued to be worn. This was determined not just by regional tradition but by religious

Duleep Singh, the Sikh maharajah of Lahore (in modern Pakistan), is shown here in 1854, in beard and turban.

Sikh Dress

Turbans and beards were always worn by men of the Sikh faith. Dress and appearance was central to Sikh religious practice, codified as the "five Ks": *kesh* (uncut hair), *kangha* (comb), *kara* (metal bangle), *kaccha* (knee-length underwear), and the *kirpan* (dagger).

The sola topi and a white service uniform are worn by a British cavalry officer during the Indian Mutiny.

dress codes. Hindu men mostly wore white cotton, often in the form of a *dhoti* (long waist cloth) or *lungi* (loincloth). Women wore the sari of cotton or silk, many in brilliant colors. Still worn today, the sari is a length of cloth folded and pleated around the waistband and draped across the shoulder.

Muslim dress was sewn and tailored, featuring trousers for both men and women. Smock-like tunics called kurtas, and wide, loose cotton trousers were commonly worn by Indians, as were turbans.

Local rulers, known as maharajahs, who often retained their titles under British rule, dressed in luxurious silks and brocades, glittering with precious jewels and gems. They also wore European dress for some formal occasions.

Sahibs and Memsahibs

The British administrators in India included military officers, police, civil servants, missionaries, and business people (known as *boxwallahs*). A strict social hierarchy existed among them. The army officers were set apart by their smart uniforms, some of which included a specifically Indian touch, such as a turban.

Both sahibs and memsahibs (gentlemen and ladies) wore full Victorian dress, with few concessions to the heat and dust other than the *sola topi* (see page 45). Riding breeches and boots were worn for travel in the jungle or for pastimes such as hunting tigers and wild pigs, or playing polo.

On a lower social scale were people of mixed Asian-European descent, who also generally favored European dress. Items of European dress were also adopted by many Indian clerks and merchants.

Southeast Asia

In the nineteenth century, much of Southeast Asia came under the rule of the French, the Dutch, and the British. The military uniforms were of those nations, but many of the Europeans were merchants or plantation owners, wearing civilian clothes. Traders introduced European manufactured textiles to the region, which were made into traditional local garments such as the wrap, or sarong.

The peoples of the region, such as the Burmese, Shan, Tai, and Khmer, had many different traditions of costume. There were the saffron robes worn by Buddhist monks; the striped wraps or sarongs woven by the Karen people on backstrap looms; and the elaborate silver headdresses of the Akha.

The Mao or Hmong wore heavy silver jewelry and costumes of black or blue, embroidered with red and pink. Tattooing was common among the Chin, while Padaung women wore neck-rings of brass-coated rattan, which elongated their necks. Female dancers at the royal court of Siam (modern-day Thailand) wore elaborate jeweled headdresses and anklets.

In Indonesia and many other parts of Southeast Asia, men and women wore sarongs. These were most commonly decorated with batik (see below).

India, especially the Gujarat region, had a fine tradition of printing elaborately patterned cotton textiles using multiple carved wooden blocks.

Batik and Sarongs

Batik is a method of dyeing cloth, long used in India, Sri Lanka, China, and Southeast Asia. It was perfected in nineteenth-century Java and other islands of modern-day Indonesia, which were then Dutch colonies.

In the 1800s, the Javanese used silks or densely woven cottons imported from India, and then after about 1815 from Europe. The cloth was prepared by washing and beating it with a wooden mallet. Batik was a wax-resist dyeing method, which means that the design was applied to the cloth in wax. When the cloth was dyed, only the unwaxed areas absorbed the pigment.

The wax design could be applied by a woman with a *canting* (a multi-spouted copper pot with a bamboo handle), or by a man with a copper stamp called a cap, introduced in the 1850s. Natural dyes included natural indigo (blue), soga bark (yellow or brown), and mengkuda leaves (red). The most extravagant batik designs used gold dust pasted and fixed to the textile.

The Far East

Cixi, dowager empress of China, wore splendid silk robes, headdresses, platform shoes, and very long fingernails.

Like Southeast Asia, the empires and kingdoms of eastern Asia were challenged by the growing power of European countries and the United States in the nineteenth century. Some tried to hold to their own cultural traditions, while others tried to adapt.

Chinese Empire

The ancient, powerful Chinese empire was in decline by the nineteenth century, as foreign powers gained control of China's ports and trade. However, China did at least retain its independence under the Qing dynasty, and also its traditional forms of dress. Since the seventeenth century, the style of costume enforced by the Qing emperors had been Manchurian (northeast Chinese) in origin. This included the long pigtail worn by all Chinese men and the long gown, or *qingpao*. Male officials wore a long costume with a round cap or conical hat and slippers.

Throughout Chinese history, dress had been carefully regulated to signify social rank. The Qing emperors wore the most splendid robes of silk, patterned with dragons. Their narrow sleeves ended in horseshoe-shaped cuffs, another Manchu fashion. Royalty and noblemen and women often grew their fingernails very long, protecting them in ornamental guards. The powerful empress dowager Cixi (1835–1908) wore her fingernails six inches (15 cm) long. She also wore very high platform shoes beneath elaborately embroidered silk robes.

Throughout nineteenth-century China, girls' feet were still cruelly bound to make them look small and dainty. Peasants, pirates on the South China Sea, and the rebel armies who repeatedly tried to expel foreigners from China, all wore simple, loose cotton trousers and jackets, often with a cloth tied around the head.

Changing Korea

For most of the nineteenth century the Korean peninsula was isolated from the outside world, and so became known internationally as "the Hermit Kingdom." Traditional Korean costume or *hanbok* was worn, with layers of long robes, wraparound skirts, and baggy trousers.

In the 1860s, Korea was attacked by France and the United States, and was threatened by Japan. The Treaty of Kanghwa (1876) compelled Korea to open its ports to foreign trade under terms favorable to Japan. Korean clothing abruptly changed to simpler and less cumbersome outfits. Jackets became shorter, with female ones now being tailored to fit the figure. Men no longer wore a topknot of hair.

This man, woman, and child wear simple, practical clothes.

Japanese Empire

Japan was also a very traditional country at the start of the nineteenth century. Men and women wore long, straight-cut robes with wide sleeves. Later in the century these became known to foreigners as kimono, meaning "clothes." The kimono was worn with a broad sash, the obi, which in this period was tied at the back rather than the front. The kimono was not practical for manual labor and so peasants and laborers wore shorter tunics and trousers. Japan looked back to the age of the samurai, the knights of medieval Japan, and soldiers wore uniforms that had barely changed since the Middle Ages.

Above: A nineteenth-century Japanese courtesan wears a red silk kimono. This form of dress was elegant and graceful.

Right: This style of kimono was adopted by the Ainu people of Japan's far north.

Beards and Lip Tattoos

The Ainu were probably the original inhabitants of Japan. By the nineteenth century they lived only in the far north, where they were continuously persecuted by their Japanese neighbors. Traditionally the Ainu made clothes from the skins of birds, seals, deer, and fox, as well as a type of barkcloth called *attush*, and ramie, a cloth made from nettle fiber. Cotton was bought from the Japanese. Ainu robes were decorated with embroidery and appliqué. Ainu men wore full beards and, for important ceremonies, wooden headdresses. The women tattooed their lips and wore embroidered headbands, earrings, and heavy necklaces.

A Tokyo street scene shows the working dress of a rickshaw man.

No foreign merchants were allowed into Japan until 1853–54, when the United States navy forced Japan to open up its ports to overseas trade. In 1868, a period of modernization began, known as the Meiji restoration. Suddenly, Western-style fashion, known as *yofuku*, became popular; it was even made compulsory for public officials. Soldiers also adopted Western-style uniforms.

Factories were built, and for the first time women were employed as workers. The kimono was not practical as working dress and was soon worn only on special days and ceremonial occasions. However, the geisha – women who entertained men – were particularly popular in the Meiji period, and they continued to wear the traditional kimono.

The Western influence on Japanese dress was reciprocated in the last years of the nineteenth century, as Japanese traditional costume began to influence fashion design in Europe.

Colonial Australia

At the start of the nineteenth century, Australia was home to about six hundred different aboriginal peoples and cultures. Most aborigines wore few clothes, but skins of wild animals, including kangaroo and opossum, provided cloaks. Also, fibers such as pandanus were woven, knotted, and dyed. Woven bags were carried over the shoulder. Bodies were decorated with scarring and painted in patterns with charcoal, white clay, or red ocher. Men's noses were sometimes pierced. Women's hair was worn long, while men's was sometimes tied up with headbands and worn with a beard.

The first Europeans to settle in Australia were the British, in 1788. By the 1800s, the official policy of befriending the aborigines was widely disregarded, and native peoples were driven off the land and often attacked and murdered. Survivors were often forced into "mission stations" and compelled to wear European dress. Some aborigines acted as guides to European explorers. Others were recruited into a Native Police Force and dressed in smart uniforms. They were used to track down criminals in remote areas and to drive out other aboriginal groups.

"PB"

The British settlement of 1788 was founded at Sydney Cove. Its aim was to establish the first of several prison

Most nineteenth-century immigrants into Australia wore European dress.

Tough working clothes and broad-brimmed hats were worn at mining camps in the Australian goldfields.

colonies. Many of the convicts from Britain and Ireland were sent here for petty crimes or political dissent. They were treated harshly and, after 1810, they wore a uniform of government issue, stamped with a broad arrow pattern, or the letters "PB," standing for "Prison Barracks." Trousers were buttoned down the sides so that leg irons could be easily fitted or removed.

New Australians

Convict transportation ended in 1840, and from then on immigration by free citizens was encouraged. Middle-class settlers wore full Victorian dress, woolen frock coats, vests, top hats, crinolines, and bonnets, despite the fierce heat in many parts of Australia.

Cities grew rapidly. By 1861, Sydney had 95,000 inhabitants, and by 1891 the population had risen to 399,000. The streets of the ports were filled with sailors from all over the world. The working classes and freed convicts dressed to suit their trades. Some lived rowdy lives and showed off their own style of clothing. These young "larrikins" wore short jackets, bell-bottom trousers, and boots with pointed toes, while their women, known as donahs, wore gaudy-colored dresses and feather boas.

The Bush Hat

Broad-brimmed hats were developed to keep off the fierce sun of the Australian bush country, and soon became a symbol of Australia itself. The most famous style sold today was first developed by an immigrant called Benjamin Dunkerley in the 1870s. It was made from felted rabbit fur and was later branded the Akubra hat.

Miners and Swagmen

Australia became a major international source of wool, which by 1885 could be shipped to London in just seventy-three days. Australian sheep farmers and cattle drovers dressed practically in boots, loose shirts, neckerchiefs, and broad-brimmed hats. Similar clothes were worn by the prospectors and miners who poured into New South Wales and Victoria in the 1850s after the discovery of gold, and by the outlaws and robbers known as bush rangers.

Migrant laborers traveled across the back country, or "outback," in search of work as sheepshearers or farm workers. They also wore hats against the sun and old working clothes. These were dusty and travel-stained, for they lived rough and camped out by night. The travelers were known as swagmen, after their "swag"—the bag of belongings they carried with them.

Many southern Chinese also traveled to Australia in the 1850s to seek work in the goldfields, where they were often attacked by racist European miners. Chinese long gowns, pigtails, and hats became a common sight on the streets of Australia.

Southern Seas

The large island of New Guinea was divided between the empires of the Dutch, the Germans, and the British in the course of the nineteenth century. Some forested highland areas remained unexplored. The native peoples wore many extraordinary costumes, decorating themselves with mud, with blue, white, or yellow clay, with feathers, cowrie shells, necklaces, ferns and leaves, and gourds. Wigs were worn for some ceremonies because it was believed that ancestors' spirits lived on in human hair. Skin was greased with pig fat or pandanus oil. Men would pierce their ears and noses and insert boar's tusks or bones in them. Women in some tribes tattooed their faces.

An itinerant "swagman," with his bundle, tells tall stories to settlers' children.

Queen Pomare ruled Polynesian Tahiti in the 1830s. She wore shifts and dresses in the European style.

grasses. Decoration included tattoos and garlands of flowers.

During the century, the Pacific islands were frequently invaded or visited by colonizers, seafarers, and Christian missionaries from France, Germany, Britain, and the United States. Shocked by the bare breasts of Polynesian women, the missionaries made many of them wear long cotton dresses in the Western style. They also discouraged tattooing, which they saw as pagan.

The Maoris

The Maori people of New Zealand were of Polynesian descent. In the nineteenth century many still wore traditional garments such as the skirt or kilt *(piupiu)*, the rain cape *(hieke* or *tureke)*, and the apron *(maro)*. They wove many different fibrous plants to make cloth, including *harakeke*, a local flax-like plant, stripping out the fiber from the stem with a shell. Capes were made from dog skin (until the breed became extinct in about 1840) and from the feathers of birds such as the kiwi. Warriors wore white feathers in their topknots and tattooed their faces in intricate, swirling patterns.

The dark-skinned Melanesian peoples of the Pacific Islands were related to those of New Guinea and they also wore shells, bones, feathers, and plant fibers.

The lighter-skinned Micronesians and Polynesians occupied most of the remaining Pacific Islands. Their traditional costume was often the *pareu*, a sort of sarong made of a barkcloth called *tapa*. Later in the century they wore pareus made from colorful traded cotton with floral designs. Skirts were made from coconut palm fronds, pandanus, and

In the 1800s, an increasing number of European whalers, outlaws, seafarers, and traders settled in New Zealand. The British declared the islands part of their empire in 1840, and settlers poured in to farm sheep and mine gold. As in Australia, the newcomers wore European dress—formal wear in town and practical farming dress in the countryside. Western (*pakeha*) dress had been widely adopted by the Maoris by the 1870s, but the traditional skills were not lost and Maori costume saw a revival for ceremonial wear in the twentieth century.

Hawaiian Islands

The Hawaiian Islands formed the northernmost settlement of the Polynesian peoples. They were united under King Kamehameha I in 1810 and became a territory of the United States at the end of the century.

In 1800 the Hawaiian population wore barkcloth in the Polynesian style. The men wore loincloths and the women wore skirts, known as *pa'u*. Western cotton textiles were soon being traded on the islands. North American missionaries arrived in 1820 and Hawaiian women adapted dresses from their Western style, using a looser, unwaisted design called the *holoku*, which literally meant "mantle." Soon, Western dress was widespread on the islands.

Foreign workers also arrived in Hawaii during the nineteenth century. The Chinese brought their traditional tunics and many set themselves up as tailors. The Japanese brought silk kimonos, the Koreans brought brightly colored short jackets, and the Filipinos introduced pina, a glossy fabric made from the fiber of the pineapple plant.

The Polynesian woman on the left wears missionary-style dress. The one on the right wears a cotton blouse with a patterned *pareu*. (The flower behind her ear indicates she is looking for a husband.)

Feathers from Paradise

The spectacular feathers of New Guinea's birds were much in demand by Western fashion designers. By the 1890s, about fifty thousand birds of paradise, which have long and brilliantly colored tails, were being exported from New Guinea each year, and were consequently threatened with extinction.

Timeline

1800s	The high-waisted "empire line" originates in France. Men begin to wear long trousers.
1800s	The start of the great age of batik dyeing in Java.
1800	The first use of the Indian word "pajama" in the English language.
1808	Dress reform is introduced in the Turkish Ottoman empire.
1820s	The rise of Gaucho costume in Argentina.
1820s	The chef's hat is introduced by Antoine Carême, in Paris.
1823	The world's first modern uniformed police force is founded in London.
1827	Maison Duvelleroy, the greatest maker of fans, opens for business in Paris.
1830	A sewing machine is patented in France.
1830s	The ready-made garment industry in the United States begins.
1832	The dress of the romantic ballet becomes popular with dancers.
1830	*Godey's Lady's Book* is first published in the United States.
1840s	The first paper patterns for home dressmaking are introduced.
1846	Charles Worth, the fashion designer, moves to Paris.
1849	Women attempt dress reform; the age of the bloomer.
1850s	The crinoline becomes a popular Western fashion.
1850s	The first khaki-colored military uniforms appear.
1855	The panama hat is exhibited at the Paris Exhibition.
1857	Garment trade workers protest in New York City.
1860	Garibaldi's Red Shirts campaign in Italy.
1863	J. B. Stetson designs his Western hat.
1870s	The decline of indigenous costume in the Americas, Africa, parts of Asia, and the Pacific islands. Western dress is adopted in many parts of the world.
1874	Levi Strauss and Jacob Davis make the first riveted jeans (waist-overalls).
1880s	The bustle, a padded backside, is a popular fashion among Western women.
1886	The "Fauntleroy" look becomes fashionable for boys.
1896	The Olympic Games are revived, coinciding with a general rise in popularity of sports and sporting outfits.

Glossary

aba The loose, flowing robes worn by Arabs.

alpaca A fine, soft woolen fiber taken from the alpaca, a relative of the llama, and the textile woven from it.

appliqué Decorative material sewn, or applied, to a background cloth.

backstrap loom A method of tensioning warp threads for weaving horizontally, by attaching them to a belt around the weaver's waist.

bandana A large kerchief, often tied around the head.

barkcloth Any fabric prepared by weaving or pounding the bark of trees.

batik A method of patterning textiles, using wax to repel dye.

bloomer A style of short dress worn over pantalettes, introduced by dress reformers in the United States in the 1840s.

boater A stiff, round, brimmed straw hat with a low crown and a ribbon hatband.

breechclout A simple cloth hanging from the waist, to cover the buttocks and genitalia.

buckskin A supple leather made from animal hide, especially deer.

bustle A pad or frame used to shape the rear of a woman's skirt in the later nineteenth century.

card Comb out and untangle fiber before spinning.

carnival A period of celebration with masks and fancy costumes, originally preceding the Christian festival of Lent.

chaps Leather coverings tied over a cowboy's trousers to protect them from thorn bushes.

clogs Wooden or wooden-soled shoes, widely worn by the working classes in nineteenth-century Europe. In French, *sabots*.

crinoline A full-skirted, bell-shaped dress supported by stiff petticoats or hoops, popular in the mid-nineteenth century.

corduroy A cotton cloth with a ridged pile, used for trousers and jackets.

corset Any garment designed to bind or give shape to the body.

cravat A broad cloth tied around the neck.

dandy A man who likes to wear the latest and most extreme fashions.

denim A heavy cotton cloth with a twill weave.

felt A cloth made from compressing wool or sometimes fur.

fez A cylindrical, tasseled hat made of red felt, commonly worn in North Africa and the Ottoman Empire.

frock coat A close-fitting, double-breasted, knee-length men's overcoat.

gaiters Buttoned or strapped coverings of the ankle or lower leg, fitting over the shoe.

gauntlets Gloves with cuffs that extend over the wrist.

habit The uniform robes worn by a monk or a nun.

kanga A printed cotton wrap worn by women, originating in nineteenth-century East Africa.

***kente* cloth** A striped cloth made from sewn strips of textile in West Africa.

kilt A short or medium-length skirt worn by men or women.

kimono Traditional Japanese robes for men and women; a term which came into use in the 1870s.

labial A plug or other ornament inserted through pierced lips or chin.

linen A textile woven from the fiber of the flax plant.

livery The uniform worn by servants of a particular noble household.

loom A frame, structure, or machine used to weave a textile.

mantilla A lacy veil worn over the head in Spanish women's costume, secured by an ornamental comb.

moccasin A soft leather slipper or shoe in the Native American style. It may be embroidered, fringed, or beaded.

mortarboard An academic cap, topped by a flat rectangle and a tassel. Also known as the Oxford cap.

muff A tube made of fur, designed to keep the hands warm.

mule A mechanical spinning machine.

muslin A fine, plain-woven cotton cloth.

panama hat A brimmed white hat, made originally in Ecuador from toquilla palm.

pandanus A family of trees and shrubs native to Southeast Asia and Oceania, providing fibrous leaves, oil, and fruit.

pantalettes Long, lacy pants worn under dresses by young Victorian women and children.

parasol A sunshade or umbrella.

pillbox hat Any hat forming a small, flat cylinder.

pinafore An apron protecting the front of the body, or a protective overdress.

pith helmet A thick but lightweight hat commonly worn by people of European descent in tropical countries. Also known as a *sola topi*.

plantation A large estate given over to the production of goods such as cotton or rubber.

ramie A textile fiber taken from a nettle-like plant of Asia.

rattan A cane obtained from the Southeast Asian climbing palm of the same name.

rivet A hammered metal fastener.

sari A rectangular cloth of cotton or silk, folded around the body to make a dress in India.

sarong A wrap of cotton or silk, originally worn by women in Southeast Asia.

satin A glossy, smooth cloth with a warp-faced weave, generally of silk.

sampler A panel of needlework displaying examples of stitching skills.

sideburns Whiskers extending from the hairline to the lower ear level, not joined to a beard.

side whiskers Extensive whiskers extending to the chin, but not joined to a beard.

snowshoe A racket-like frame of wood and thongs, which distributes the weight of the body when walking over soft snow.

sola topi See "pith helmet."

sombrero A hat of Central America, with a wide brim.

spur A metal point fitted to the heel of the boot, used to urge on a horse.

stock A band-like neck-cloth.

sweatshops Workshops where people work long hours for low pay.

tailcoat A coat with long flaps extending to the rear of the calf.

tartan plaid A cross-barred patterned cloth originating in Scotland and indicating membership of a clan.

textile Any cloth produced by weaving.

topknot A long lock of hair worn at the crown of the head.

toque A brimless cap, especially the tall, white one worn by chefs.

tortoiseshell A mottled, horny substance, yellow and brown, made from the shell of a marine turtle.

Tracht Regional folk costume in German-speaking lands.

train Part of a dress which trails behind the wearer.

trousseau The clothes and linen brought to a household by a newly married bride.

turban Headgear made by winding a cloth around a cap or directly around the head.

tulle A fine, gauzy silk.

twill A weave in which warp and weft form diagonal parallel lines, as in cloths such as serge.

vestments The ritual clothes worn by priests.

whalebone A pliable, horny substance found in the mouths of some whales and used in corsetry.

wimple A linen garment covering head and neck, which by the nineteenth century was worn only by nuns.

yarn Thread used in weaving or knitting.

Further Information

General Reference Sources

Beaudouin-Ross, Jacqueline, *Form and Fashion: Nineteenth Century Montreal Dress* (McGill-Queen's University Press, 1992)

Blum, Stella, *Fashions and Costumes from Godey's Lady's Book* (Dover Publications, 1985)

Leniston, Florence, *Elegant French Fashions of the Late Nineteenth Century* (Dover Publications, 1997)

Norris, Herbert, and Curtis, Oswald, *Nineteenth Century Costume and Fashion* (Dover Publications, 1998)

Peacock, John, *The Chronicle of Western Costume: From the Ancient World to the Late Twentieth Century* (Thames and Hudson, 2003)

Willett Cunnington, C., *Fashion and Women's Attitudes in the Nineteenth Century* (Dover Publications, 2003)

Internet Resources

http://www.costumes.org/history/100pages/victlinks.htm
Has a huge and useful range of links.

http://members.aol.com/nebula5/tcpinfo3.html
Costume page: ethnic and folk costume links.

http://www.costumes.org/history/100pages/regencylinks.htm
Regency and Empire clothing links.

http://locutus.ucr.edu/~cathy/reg3.html
The Regency Fashion Page.

http://www.songsmyth.com/costumerscompanion.html
Jessamyn's Regency Costume Companion.

http://www.marquise.de/en/1800/index.shtml
La Couturière Parisienne: 1800s.

http://www.levistrauss.com/
Levi Strauss and Co.

http://inventors.about.com/library/inventors/blindustrialrevolutiontextiles.htm
The Industrial Revolution—a timeline of textile machinery.

http://www.textile.unsw.edu.au/Fax%26Fix/TextHist/History.htm
A history of textiles.

http://dept.kent.edu/museum/costume/bonc/3timesearch/tsnineteenth/19.html
Bissonnette on Costume Time Search: the Nineteenth Century.

Index

Page numbers in bold refer to illustrations.

aprons 11, 15, 19, 28, 29, 30, 31, 37, 39, 58

bathing costumes 38, **38**
belts 13, 15, 20, 21, 31
blankets 6, 16, 17, 18, 21, **21**
bloomers 10, **10,** 60, 61
blouses 9, 28, 30, **30,** 31, 49, 59
   huipils 21
bodices 28, 29, 30, 31
body painting 21, 55
body piercing 55, 57
breechclouts (loincloths) 14, 17, 47, 59, 61
   lungi 50
breeches 8, 19, 25, 33, 38, 39, 42, 50
   knickerbockers 43
   lederhosen 28
bustles 8, 24, 60, 61

capes 11, 24, 25, 27, 31, 41, 49, 58
chaps 14, 61
children's clothing 42–3
cloaks 10, 15, 16, 20, 21, **21,** 25, 31, 41, 47, 55
coats 6, 15, 19, 31
   frock coats 24, 34, 44, 56, 61
   overcoats 17, 31
   tailcoats 8, 12, 22, 41, 46, 62
corsets 8–9, 61
crinolines 8, 12, 24, 38, 56, 60, 61

dresses 8, 11, **11,** 12, 13, 14, 15, 17, 19, 25, 26, 27, 28, 29, 37, 39, 40, 41, 43, 45, 49, 56, 58, **58,** 59, **59**
   dirndl 29
   empire line 24, **24,** 43, 60
dyes and dyeing 5, 14, 21, 23, 27, 46, 48
   batik 51, 60, 61

embroidery 11, 22, 26, 29, 30, 31, 34, 51, 52, 54

fans 25, **25,** 60
feathers 5, 6, 14, 15, 16, 21, 29, 30, 31, 47, 48, 49, 56, 57, 58, 59
footwear
   boots 8, 9, 14, 15, 17, 18, 19, **19,** 20, 24, 25, 27, 28, 30, 31, 39, 41, 42, 44, 46, 50, 56, 57
   clogs 22, 25, 28, 61
   moccasins 14, **14,** 17, 61
   sandals 17, 20
   slippers 8, 17, 25, 31, 47, 52
   snowshoes 19, 62

gaiters 8, 34, 39, 46, 61
gauntlets 15, 61
gowns 20, 22, 34, 35, 57
   qingpao 52

hairstyles 8, 14, 17, **17,** 20, 24, 27, 30, 31, 41, 49, 52, 53, 54, 55, 57
   hanbok 53
hats 6, 12, 15, 16, 17, 18, 19, 20, 21, 25, 26, 29, 30, 31, 32, 35, 36, 39, 46, 49, 52, 56, 57
   boaters 39, 61
   bonnets 9, 10, 11, 12, 14, 15, 19, 37, 38, 43, 56
   bush hats 57
   caps 19, 20, 22, 26, 34, 35, 37, 38, 43, 46, 52
   cocked hats 41
   derbies 9
   fezes 46, 49, 61
   kèpis 36, 46, **46**
   panamas 20, 60, 62
   peaked caps 18, 28, 31, 38, 39, 45
   pillboxes 9, 18, 18, 35, 62
   sombreros 14, 20, 62
   Stetsons 14, 60
   straw hats 9, 12, 15, 28, 42, 43
   streimels 30
   top hats 9, 12, 24, 41, 56
   toque blanches 32, **32,** 60, 62
headwear
   agal 49
   bandanas 17, 20, 61
   headbands 17, 47, 54, 55
   head cloths 20
   headdresses 14, 16, 21, 25, **25,** 28, 31, 37, 47, 51, 54
   headscarves 12, 27, 31
   mantillas 20, **20,** 25, 61
   turbans 12, 13, 44, 49, 50, **50,** 62
   veils 20, 25, 26, 35, 37, 49
   wigs 33, 35, 57
   wimples 37, 62
   yarmulkes 30
helmets
   Pickelhaubes 29, 36
   sola topis 45, **45,** 50, **50,** 62

jackets 6, 8, 9, 10, 11, 12, 15, 18, 19, 25, 32, 43, 46, 49, 53, 56, 59
   blazers 38, 39
jewelry 13, 16, 18, 27, 41, 47, 48, 49, 50, 51, 54

kangas 47, 61

leggings 13, 14, 26
leotards 41

makeup 41
masks 13, 48
muffs 8, 62

neckerchiefs 14, 32, 57

pajamas 44, 60
pinafores 19, 43, 62
Podhale costume 31
ponchos 20, 21

ribbons 8, 9, 22, 24, 25, 27, 28, 31, 40
robes 33, 34, 42, 46, 49, 51, 52, 53
   kimonos 54, **54,** 55, 59, 61

saris 50, 62
sarongs 51, 62
pareus 58, 59
sashes 21, 27, 31, 40, 46–7, 49, 54
scarves 40
   puggarrees 45, 45
shawls 10, 15, 21, 25, 31
shifts 20, 58
shirts 8, 11, 12, 13, 14, 15, 17, 20, 22, 24, 27, 30, 41, 45, 46, 57
skirts 8, 9, 12, 13, 15, 16, 18, 20, 21, 28, 29, 30, 31, 39, 40, 49, 53, 58, 59
   kilts 16, 26, 43, 58, 61
socks 18, 29
spurs 15, 20, 62
stockings 8, 25, 33, 39, 43
stocks 8, 24, 62
suits 9, 38, 39
   sailor suits 42, **42**
sweaters 33, **33,** 38, 39, 43

tassels 26, 28, 31, 38, 46
tattooing 51, 54, 57, 58
   Tracht 28–9, 62
trousers 8, 9, 10, 12, 14, 15, 18, 19, 20, 27, 28, 30, 31, 39, 43, 44, 46, 49, 50, 53, 54, 56, 60
   jeans 16, 60
tunics 17, 19, 21, **21,** 28, 31, 42, 44, 54, 59
   kurtas 50
tutus 40

underwear 40
   drawers 43
   pantelettes 42, 43, 62
   petticoats 43
uniforms 7, 15, 19, 22–3, 29, 32–3, 35, 36–7, 46, 50, 51, 54, 55, 56, 60

vestments 34, 34, 62
vests 8, 9, 11, 12, 24, 27, 30, 31, 41, 46, 49, 56